Irishmen United

Society of United Irishmen of Dublin

Established November IX, MDCCXCI.

Irishmen United

Society of United Irishmen of Dublin
Established November IX, MDCCXCI.

ISBN/EAN: 9783337126247

Printed in Europe, USA, Canada, Australia, Japan

Cover: Foto ©Andreas Hilbeck / pixelio.de

More available books at **www.hansebooks.com**

SOCIETY

OF

UNITED IRISHMEN

OF

DUBLIN.

ESTABLISHED
NOVEMBER IX. MDCCXCI.

"LET THE NATION STAND."

—DUBLIN:—

1794.

CONTENTS.

			Page
1791			
Nov.	9.	Association and declaration of the Society, -	[illegible]
		Test, - -	5
Dec.	30.	Circular letter, -	6
1792			
Feb.	25.	Resolutions respecting undefined privilege, -	12
		Letter to the Society of United Irishmen at Belfast,	13
March	30.	Letter from Mr. Tandy,	15
		And resolutions consequent thereon,	17
Sep.	14.	Address to the nation,	18

CONTENTS.

Page

Oct. 26. Address to the friends of the people at London, 29

Nov. 3. Letter to the Chairman, from Thomas Braughal, Esq. with the resolutions of the Catholic meeting, 30

23. Address to the delegates for reform in Scotland, 32

30. Circular letter to the different Societies of United Irishmen, 40

Dec. 7. Resolution relative to the Catholic Convention. 42

14. Address to the Volunteers of Ireland, * 43

23. Resolutions relative to that Address, 48

1793

Jan. 11. Resolution expressing gratitude to the King for a part of his speech from the throne, 50

25. Address to the Irish Nation, 51

Feb. 80. Report on the War, the Militia and the Gunpowder Act, 62

* *For the supposed distribution of this address, an information ex officio was filed against Archibald Hamilton Rowan, Esq. and he was sentenced to pay a fine of* 500l. *and to be imprisoned for two years, commencing* 29*th January* 1794. *See the report of the trial published by Byrne.*

CONTENTS.

		Page
Feb. 24. and March 1.	Proceedings againſt the Hon. Simon Butler and Oliver Bond, Eſq. in the Houſe of Lords, and reſolutions of the Society on the Secret Committee, -	67
	Reſolution of attachment to the officers of the Society,	72
2.	Their anſwer,	73
3.	Addreſs to the people of Ireland, - -	74
June 7.	Addreſs to our Catholic Countrymen, -	81
21.	Addreſs to Ireland,	86
July 15.	Reſolutions on the Convention Bill, - -	91
26.	Proceedings relative to Henry Sheares, Eſq. - -	94
Aug. 12.	Addreſs to James Reynolds, M. D. - -	98
	His anſwer, -	99
16.	Addreſs to the Hon. Simon Butler and Oliver Bond, Eſq. on their enlargement	100

CONTENTS.

		Page
	Their anſwer, -	104
Oct. 28.	Proceedings in Edinburgh, againſt Archibald Hamilton Rowan, -	105
Nov. 22.	Addreſs to Thomas Muir,	117
25.	Reſolutions of the Britiſh Convention, -	121
	Addreſs to the Britiſh Convention, - -	122
	PLAN OF REFORM, and addreſs to the people thereon,	124
1794		
Feb. 7.	Addreſs to Archibald Hamilton Rowan, -	131
8.	His anſwer, -	133
	Proceedings in the caſe of Mr. Tandy, 26th June, 1792. -	135
March 14.	Addreſs to the people in juſtification of the Plan of Reform.	190
	CONSTITUTION OF THE SOCIETY.	199

Page

March 10. Anſwer of Thomas Muir, 203

1792.

June 22. Reſolutions reſpecting James Napper Tandy, 205

Nov. 16. Anſwer to Thomas Braughal, Chairman of the Catholic meeting, - 206

1793.

Dec. 20. Reſolutions reſpecting the Britiſh Convention. 207

SOCIETY

OF

UNITED IRISHMEN.

EAGLE, *Euſtace-ſtreet*, 9th of *November*, 1791.

AT A MEETING

OF THE

SOCIETY OF UNITED IRISHMEN

OF

DUBLIN,

The Hon. SIMON BUTLER in the Chair,

The following was agreed to:

WHEN we reflect how often the Freemen and Freeholders of Dublin have been convened, humbly to expreſs their Grievances to Parliament —how often they have ſolicited the enaction of good, and the repeal of bad Laws—how often, for ſucceſſive years, they have petitioned againſt the obnoxious and unconſtitutional Police Act, and how often all theſe applications have been treated with the moſt perfect contumacy and

A

contempt.—When these facts are brought to recollection, is there an Honest Man will say, that the House of Commons have the smallest respect for the People, or believe themselves their Legitimate Representatives?—The fact is, that the great Majority of that House, consider themselves as the Representatives of their own Money, or the hired servants of the English Government, whose Minister here, is appointed for the sole purpose of dealing out Corruption to them—at the expence of Irish Liberty, Irish Commerce, and Irish Improvement.—This being the case, it naturally follows, that such Minister is not only the representative of the English Views against this Country, but is also *The sole Representative of the People of Ireland.* To elucidate which assertion, it is only necessary to ask, whether a single question in favour of this oppressed Nation can be carried without HIS Consent?——and whether any measure, however inimical, may not through HIS influence be effected?

IN this state of abject Slavery, no hope remains for us, but in the sincere and hearty *Union of All the People*, for a compleat and radical reform of Parliament; because it is obvious, that *one Party alone* have been ever unable to obtain a single Blessing for their Country; and the Policy of our Rulers has been always such, as to keep the different Sects at variance, in which they have been but too well seconded by our own folly.

FOR the attainment then of this great and important object—for the removal of absurd and ruinous distinctions—and for promoting a complete Coalition of the People—a Society has been formed, composed of all Religious Persuasions, who have adopted for their Name,——THE SOCIETY OF UNITED IRISHMEN OF DUBLIN,—and have taken as their

DECLARATION.

That of a ſimilar Society in BELFAST, which is as follows:

"IN the preſent great æra of reform, when unjuſt Governments are falling in every quarter of Europe; when religious perſecution is compelled to abjure her tyranny over conſcience; when the Rights of Men are aſcertained in theory, and that theory ſubſtantiated by practice; when antiquity can no longer defend abſurd and oppreſſive forms againſt the common ſenſe and common intereſts of mankind; when all Government is acknowledged to originate from the People, and to be ſo far only obligatory as it protects their rights and promotes their welfare; we think it our duty, as Iriſhmen, to come forward, and ſtate what we feel to be our heavy grievance, and what we know to be its effectual remedy.

WE HAVE NO NATIONAL GOVERNMENT— We are ruled by Engliſhmen, and the ſervants of Engliſhmen; whoſe object is the intereſt of another country; whoſe inſtrument is corruption; whoſe ſtrength is the weakneſs of Ireland; and theſe men have the whole of the power and patronage of the Country, as means to ſeduce and ſubdue the honeſty and the ſpirit of her Repreſentatives in the Legiſlature. Such an extrinſic power, acting with uniform force in a direction too frequently oppoſite to the true line of our obvious intereſts, can be reſiſted with effect ſolely by *unanimity, deciſion, and ſpirit in the People*; qualities which may be exerted moſt legally, conſtitutionally and efficaciouſly, by that great meaſure eſſential to the proſperity and freedom of Ireland, AN EQUAL REPRESENTATION OF ALL THE PEOPLE IN PARLIAMENT.

" We do not here mention as grievances the rejection of a Place-Bill, of a Pension-Bill, of a Responsibility-Bill; the sale of Peerages in one House; the corruption publickly avowed in the other; nor the notorious infamy of Borough traffic between both; not that we are insensible of their enormity, but that we consider them as but symptoms of that mortal disease, which corrodes the vitals of our Constitution, and leaves to the People in their own Government but the shadow of a name.

IMPRESSED with these sentiments we have agreed to form an Association, to be called, THE SOCIETY OF UNITED IRISHMEN: and we do pledge ourselves to our Country, and mutually to each other, that we will steadily support and endeavour by all due means to carry into effect the following resolutions:

" I. RESOLVED, That the weight of English Influence, in the Government of this Country, is so great as to require a Cordial Union among ALL THE PEOPLE OF IRELAND, to maintain that balance which is essential to the preservation of our Liberties, and the extension of our Commerce.

" II. THAT the sole constitutional mode by which this influence can be opposed, is by a compleat and radical reform of the Representation of the People in Parliament.

" III. THAT no Reform is practicable, efficacious, or just, which shall not include *Irishmen* of every Religious Persuasion.

" SATISFIED as we are, that the intestine divisions among Irishmen, have too often given encouragement and impunity to audacious and corrupt administrations, in measures which, but for these divisions they durst not have attempted, we submit our Resolutions to the Nation, as the basis of our Political Faith.

" WE have gone to what we conceive to be the root of the evil; we have ſtated what we conceive to be the remedy.—With a Parliament thus reformed, every thing is eaſy; without it, nothing can be done. And we do call on, and moſt earneſtly exhort our Countrymen in general to follow our example, and form ſimilar ſocieties in every quarter of the Kingdom for the promotion of conſtitutional knowledge, the abolition of bigotry in religion and politics, and the equal diſtribution of the Rights of Man through all Sects and Denominations of Iriſhmen.

" THE People when thus collected will feel their own weight, and ſecure that power which theory has already admitted as their portion, and to which if they be not arouſed by their preſent provocations to vindicate it, they deſerve to forfeit their pretenſions FOR EVER.

JAMES NAPPER TANDY, *Secretary*.

T E S T.

I A. B. *in the preſence of God, do pledge myſelf to my country, that I will uſe all my abilities and influence in the attainment of an impartial and adequate repreſentation of the Iriſh Nation in Parliament—And as a means of abſolute and immediate neceſſity in the eſtabliſhment of this Chief Good of Ireland, I will endeavour, as much as lies in my ability, to forward a brotherhood of affection, an identity of intereſts, a communion of rights, and an union of power among Iriſhmen of all religious perſuaſions; without which every reform in parliament muſt be partial, not national, inadequate to the wants, deluſive to the wiſhes, and inſufficient for the freedom and happineſs of this Country.*

Friday, 30th December, 1791.

SOCIETY OF UNITED IRISHMEN OF DUBLIN.

The Hon. SIMON BUTLER in the Chair.

RESOLVED, UNANIMOUSLY, *That the following Circular Letter, reported by our Committee of Correſpondence, be adopted and printed.*

THIS Letter is addreſſed to you from the Correſponding Committee of the Society of United Iriſhmen in Dublin.

We annex the Declaration of Political Principles which we have ſubſcribed, and the Teſt which we have taken, as a ſocial and ſacred compact to bind us more cloſely together.

The object of this Inſtitution is to make an United Society of the Iriſh Nation; to make all Iriſhmen—Citizens;—all Citizens—Iriſhmen; nothing appearing to us more natural at all times, and at this criſis of Europe more ſeaſonable, than that thoſe who have common intereſts, and common enemies, who ſuffer common wrongs, and lay claim to common rights, ſhould know each other and ſhould act together. In our opinion ignorance has been the Demon of diſcord, which has ſo long deprived Iriſhmen, not only of the bleſſings of well regulated government, but even the common benefits of civil ſociety. Peace in this iſland has hitherto been a peace on the principles and with the conſequences of civil war. For a century paſt there has indeed been tranquility, but to moſt of our dear countrymen it has been the tranquility of a dungeon; and if the land has lately profpered, it has been owing to the goodnefs of Providence, and the ftrong efforts of Human Nature refifting and overcoming the malignant influence of a miferable adminiftration.

To refift this influence, which rules by difcord and embroils by fyftem, it is vain to act as individuals or as parties;—It becomes neceffary by an union of minds, and a knowledge of each other, to will and to act as a nation. To know each other is to know ourfelves—the weaknefs of one and the ftrength of many. Union, therefore, is power—it is wifdom—it muft prove liberty.

Our defign, therefore, in forming this Society, is to give an example, which, when well followed, muft collect the public will, and concentrate the public power, into one folid mafs the effect; of which once put in motion, muft be rapid, momentous, and confequential.

In thus affociating we have thought little about our anceftors—much of our pofterity. Are we for ever to walk like beafts of prey, over fields which thefe anceftors ftained with blood? In looking back, we fee nothing on the one part but favage force fucceeded by favage policy; on the other, an unfortunate nation "fcattered and peeled, meted out and trodden down!" We fee a mutual intolerance, and a common carnage of the firft moral emotions of the heart, which lead us to efteem and place confidence in our fellows creatures. We fee this, and are filent. But we gladly look forward to brighter profpects—to a People united in the fellowfhip of freedom—to a Parliament the exprefs image of that People—to a profperity eftablifhed on civil, political, and religious Liberty—to a Peace—not the gloomy and precarious ftillnefs of men brooding over their wrongs, but that ſtable Tranquility which reſts on the rights of human nature, and leans on the arms by which theſe rights are to be maintained.

Our principal rule of conduct has been, to attend to thoſe things in which we agree, to exclude from our thoughts thoſe in which we differ. We agree in knowing what are our rights, and in daring to aſſert them. If the rights of men be duties to God, we are in this reſpect of one religion. Our creed of civil faith is the ſame. We agree in thinking that there is not an individual among our millions, whoſe happineſs can be eſtabliſhed on any foundation ſo rational and ſo ſolid, as on the happineſs of the whole community—We agree, therefore, in the neceſſity of giving political value and ſtation to the great majority of the people; and we think that whoever deſires an amended Conſtitution, without including the great body of the people, muſt on his own principles be convicted of political perſecution, and political monopoly. If the preſent electors be themſelves a morbid part of our conſtitution, where are we to recur for redreſs but to the whole community? "A more unjuſt and abſurd conſtitution cannot be deviſed, than that which condemns the natives of a country to perpetual ſervitude, under the arbitrary dominion of ſtrangers and ſlaves."

We agree in thinking, that the firſt and moſt indiſpenſable condition of the laws in a free ſtate, is the aſſent of thoſe whoſe obedience they require, and for whoſe benefit only they are deſigned. Without, therefore, an impartial and adequate Repreſentation of the community, we agree in declaring, We can have no conſtitution—no Country—no Ireland. Without this, our late revolution we declare to be fallacious and ideal; a thing much talked of, but neither felt nor ſeen. The act of Iriſh Sovereignty has been merely toſſed out of the Engliſh Houſes into the Cabinet of the Miniſter; and nothing remains to the People, who of right are every thing, but a ſervile Majeſty and a ragged Independence.

We call moſt earneſtly on every great and good Man, who at the late æra ſpoke or acted for his Country, to conſider leſs of what was done than of what there remains to do. We call upon their ſenatorial wiſdom to conſider the monſtrous and immeaſurable diſtance which ſeparates, in this iſland, the ranks of ſocial life, makes labour ineffectual, taxation unproductive, and divides the nation into petty deſpotiſm and public miſery. We call upon their tutelar genius, to remember, that government is inſtituted to remedy, not to render more grievous the natural inequality of mankind, and that unleſs the rights of the whole community be aſſerted, anarchy (we cannot call it government) muſt continue to prevail, where the ſtrong tyrannize, the rich oppreſs, and the maſs are brayed in a mortar. We call upon them, therefore, to build their arguments and their actions on the broad platform of general good.

Let not the rights of nature be enjoyed merely by connivance, and the rights of conſcience merely by toleration. If you raiſe up a prone people, let it not be merely to their knees. Let the nation ſtand. Then will it caſt away the bad habit of ſervitude, which has brought with it indolence, ignorance, an extinction of our faculties, an abandonment of our very nature. Then will every right obtained, every franchiſe exerciſed, prove a ſeed of ſobriety, induſtry, and regard to character, and the manners of the people will be formed on the model of their free conſtitution.

This rapid expoſition of our principles, our object, and our rule of conduct, muſt naturally ſuggeſt the wiſh of multiplying ſimilar Societies, and the propriety of addreſſing ſuch a deſire to you. Is it neceſſary for us to requeſt, that you will hold out your Hand, and open your heart to your Countrymen, Townſman, Neighbour?—Can you form a hope for political redemption, and by political penalties, or civil excommunications, withhold the Rights of Nature from your Brother? We beſeech you to rally all the Friends of Liberty within your circle round a Society of this kind as a centre. Draw together your beſt and braveſt thoughts, your beſt and braveſt men. You will experience, as we have done, that theſe Points of Union will quickly attract numbers, while the aſſemblage of ſuch Societies, acting in concert, moving as one body, with one impulſe and one direction, will, in no long time, become not parts of the nation, but the nation itſelf; ſpeaking with its voice, expreſſing its will, reſiſtleſs in its power. We again entreat you to look around for Men fit to form thoſe ſtable Supports on which Ireland may reſt the Lever of Liberty. If there be but Ten, take thoſe Ten. If there be but Two, take thoſe Two, and truſt with confidence to the ſincerity of your intention, the juſtice of your cauſe, and the ſupport of your Country.

Two objects intereſt the Nation—A Plan of Repreſentation—and the means of accompliſhing it.—Theſe ſocieties will be a moſt powerful means. But a popular Plan would itſelf be a means for its own accompliſhment. We have, therefore, to requeſt, that you will favour us with your ideas reſpecting the Plan which appears to you most eligible and practicable, on the present more enlarged and liberal principles which actuate the People; at the same time giving your sentiments upon our National Coalition, on the means of promoting it, and on the political state and disposition of the county or town where you reside. We know what resistance will be made to your patriotic efforts by those who triumph in the disunion and degradation of their Country. The greater the necessity for reform, the greater probably will be the resistance. We know that there is much spirit that requires being brought into mass, as well as much massy body that must be refined into spirit. We have many enemies, and no enemy is contemptible. We do not despise the enemies of the Union, the Liberty and the Peace of Ireland, but we are not of a nature, nor have we encouraged the habit of fearing any Man, or any Body of Men, in an honest and honourable cause. In great undertakings like the present, we declare that we have found it always more difficult to attempt, than to accomplish. The people of Ireland must perform all that they wish, if they attempt all that they can.

Signed by Order,

JAMES NAPPER TANDY, *Sec*

To whom Letters on this subject are to be addressed

February 25, 1792.

SOCIETY OF UNITED IRISHMEN OF DUBLIN.

ARCHIBALD HAMILTON ROWAN, Esq. in the Chair;

(*The* HON. SIMON BUTLER *having been, from motives of personal delicacy, requested to leave it.*)

RESOLVED UNANIMOUSLY,

I. THAT the exercise of undefined privilege is as dangerous to the Liberty of the Subject, as the exercise of unlimited prerogative and equally unrecognized by the true spirit of the Laws and Constitution.

II. THAT having associated for the attainment of great national objects, and to promote union among Irishmen of all religious persuasions, this Society is entitled to the respect, which objects of such importance naturally claim.

III. THAT *an insolent menace* having been publicly thrown out, respecting this Society, We think it incumbent on us to declare that we do not shrink from, but anxiously desire to meet any constitutional inquiry into our principles and conduct; and reserving for that occasion the justification of our actions, we resign to merited contempt, *the scorn of official station*, or the scoff of *unprincipled venality*.

IV. That Five Thouſand Copies of our Declaration and Circular Letter, with theſe Reſolutions, be printed and diſtributed by our Committee of Correſpondence.

By order of the Society,

THEO. WOLFE TONE, *Pro. Sec.*

TO THE SOCIETY OF UNITED IRISHMEN IN BELFAST.

PROMPTED by Duty as well as Inclination to make always an early Anſwer to your Letters, our Delay in the preſent Inſtance was at firſt occaſioned by trivial Circumſtances, made important merely by their Number, but latterly has been owing to a ſimple and a ſerious Cauſe.—The compelled Abſence of our Secretary Mr. NAPPER TANDY, a Man who with an erect Mind, and an honeſt Heart, has during a long courſe of Years, ſtem'd the torrent of corruption, in the midſt of a corrupt City; who at the Riſk even of his Popularity the ſole Reward of a Life ſpent in the public ſervice, entered with Ardour into your ſcheme of coaleſcing all religious Perſuaſions in the Unity of a common Cauſe; and who, if he now ſuffers, has the Conſolation to think that he ſuffers in common with Magna Charta. The fundamental Principles of the Conſtitution are violated in his Perſon: the perſonal Liberty of the Subject is laid proſtrate at the Mercy of a Reſolution of one branch of Legiſlature, the priva lex becomes equivalent to an act of Legiſlation: Proclamation foreruns law, anticipates its Judgment and Magna Charta is thus crucified between the two thieves of the Common Right, Privilege on the one hand, and Prerogative on the other. While we are thinking of Elective Franchise and Political Power, let us take heed that we are not losing even civil Liberty, and that a custom of Parliament does not operate as a real Lettre de Cachet, against Personal Security and freedom. Whether the Jurisdiction which the House of Commons, has over its own members, or the privileges which shields them from the abuse of Prerogative, should be converted into an omnipotent instrument of ministerial Vengeance against the people, stretching its Arm across the Nation, and suspending the natural Process of Law, (all Crimes being cognizable in their proper Courts) whether such a power not founded on any Principle, not defined by any rule, and justified only by occasional practice, be consistent with the Liberty of the Nation, the sacred trial by jury, the law of the land, judge ye! We shall only ask what is tyranny but the oppressive and injurious exertion of unconstitutional and indefinite Authority, where they who do Injustice commit it with Impunity, and he who suffers it, is without Redress, however Innocent he may be, however Meritorious. We join with you in thinking that the reciprocal Admission of Members subject to the Regulations you mention would serve to draw the bonds of political Brotherhood more closely between our Societies, and the adoption of such a Seal as you have described has the stamp of our approbation.

February 28th, 1792.

Friday, March 30, 1792.

SOCIETY OF UNITED IRISHMEN.

The Hon. SIMON BUTLER in the Chair.

The following Letter was read from the Chair.

MY DEAR SIR,

I HAVE to requeſt that you will be ſo good as to lay the following Circumſtances before the Society of United Iriſhmen, as the Cauſe of my Abſence from that moſt reſpectable Body:

On the 22d Day of Feb. laſt, a Complaint having been made to the Houſe of Commons by one of its Members, of a Breach of Privilege committed by me, the Houſe, without ſummoning me to anſwer the Complaint, ordered that I ſhould be immediately taken into Cuſtody of the Serjeant at Arms, and brought forthwith to the Bar of the Houſe. The Serjeant at Arms informed the Houſe, that he had diſpatched three of the Meſſengers attending the Houſe to execute the Order for taking me into his Cuſtody; one of whom being brought to the Bar, informed the Houſe, that he went to the Houſe of Mr. James Tandy, in Chancery-lane, where he arreſted me, and ſhewed me the Warrant and his Authority; that I went into a Parlour, as if for my Hat, but ſhut the Door, and made my Eſcape, as he ſuppoſed, through a Window. The houſe then reſolved, that I, having been arreſted by a Warrant from Mr. Speaker, iſſued by the Order of the Houſe, and having made my Eſcape from the Officer of the Houſe who arreſted me, was guilty of a groſs Violation of the Privileges of the Houſe, and reſolved, that an humble Addreſs be preſented to the Lord Lieutenant, that he would be graciouſly pleaſed to direct, that a Proclamation might iſſue for apprehending me, with a Promiſe of Reward for the ſame, and that ſaid Addreſs be forthwith preſented to the Lord Lieutenant by ſuch Members of the Houſe as were of his Majeſty's Moſt Hon. Privy Council. The Addreſs having been accordingly preſented by the Houſe to the Lord Lieutenant, a Proclamation was inſtantly iſſued by the Lord Lieutenant and Council for apprehending me, with a Promiſe of Reward for the ſame. The Proclamation recites the Information given to the Houſe by the Serjeant at Arms and Meſſenger, and the Reſolution of the Houſe, ſubſequent to the ſame, but does not ſet forth the original Complaint, or the immediate Order in Conſequence thereof; but directs the Perſon who ſhould apprehend me, to carry me before ſome of the Juſtices of the Peace, or Chief Magiſtrates of the County, Town, or Place where I ſhould be apprehended, who are reſpectively required to ſecure me, and thereof given ſpeedy Notice to the Speaker of the Houſe, the Serjeant at Arms attending the ſaid Houſe, and to the Clerk of the Council, to the End that I might be forthcoming to be dealt with or proceeded againſt according to Law; and for Prevention of my Eſcape into Parts beyond Seas, it commands all Officers of the Cuſtoms, and other Officers and Subjects, of and in the reſpective Ports and maratime Towns and Places within the Kingdom, to be careful and diligent in the Examination of all Perſons that ſhall paſs or endeavour to paſs beyond the Seas; and it alſo ſtrictly commands all Perſons, as they will anſwer the contrary at their

Perils, not any ways to conceal, but to discover me, to the End that I may be secured.

I have the Honour to be,
Dear Sir,
Very truly and sincerely yours,

March JAMES NAPPER TANDY.
26, 1792.

P. S. I enclose you the Proclamation and Votes.

To the Hon. Simon Butler, President Society of United Irishmen.

The foregoing Letter was ordered to be entered on the Journals of the Society.

RESOLVED, UNANIMOUSLY, That the Power assumed by the House of Commons to order the Serjeant at Arms to take into Custody a Subject of this Realm, not a member of that House, upon a Complaint made by one of its Members of a Breach of Privilege, without summoning the Party complained of, to answer the Complaint, is unwarranted by the Laws of the Land.

RESOLVED, UNANIMOUSLY, That the Proclamation issued in this Case is not warranted by Law.

RESOLVED, UNANIMOUSLY, That the Liberty of the Subject is violated in the Person of Mr. Tandy, that his Cause must now be considered as that of the Public, and brought forward to receive a judicial Decision.

RESOLVED, UNANIMOUSLY, That a Committee of Secrecy be appointed to carry the last mentioned Resolution into Effect, and impowered to draw upon the Treaſurer for ſuch Sums as it may require for that Purpoſe.

Signed by Order,

THEO. WOLFE TONE, *Pro. Sec.*

September 14*th.* 1792.

SOCIETY OF UNITED IRISHMEN OF DUBLIN.

The Hon. SIMON BUTLER in the Chair.

THE FOLLOWING

ADDRESS

WAS UNANIMOUSLY AGREED TO FROM THIS SOCIETY

TO THE NATION.

WE obſerve with concern and indignation the inſidious means employed to ſtifle the Catholic Voice in its humble repreſentation of the Grievances which afflict the people, and of the Remedy ſpecified to redreſs them. We lament that men of any pretenſions to common ſenſe and public ſpirit ſhould have been blindly ſeduced into the publication of the moſt flagrant abſurdities, calumnies, and libels, againſt the moſt oppreſſed, patient, and numerous deſcription of our Fellow Citizens. That ſuch publications ſhould have iſſued from the Grand-Jury-Room cannot be matter of ſurprize. Since the nomination of Sheriffs has been transferred from the people to the Crown, Grand Juries, which are returnable by these officers, have lost their original character of Independence, and are now notoriously subordinate to Aristocratic Intrigue and Ministerial Corruption. As therefore these ancient bodies, which should be the sacred Organs of Truth, as well as the Guardians of the Constitution, have in this instance degenerated into instruments of prejudice and civil dissention, we feel it a duty which we owe to public justice as well as to our country, to appeal from the unjust sentence of a few influenced men to the Tribunal of a rational Nation.

It appears that a small dispersed number of Individuals of the Catholic persuasion, without authority from the body at large, were, in the course of last Session, cajoled into the measure of presenting an eleemosynary Address to Government, and this was craftily made the vehicle of some obscure and ill-founded censure upon the constitutional conduct of the Catholic Committee. The embarrassment occasioned by this stale artifice, determined the Committee to obtain an unequivocal expression of the Catholic sentiment; and with this view they printed, published, and circulated throughout Ireland several thousand copies of a Letter, submitting to the Catholic people a Plan for electing Delegates to the General Committee: a Plan at once the most simple, orderly, and the best calculated for framing an unquestionable organ of public opinion. The Letter solicits the attendance of Delegates appointed for the express purpose and with the express instruction of IMPLORING and SUPPLICATING from the Legislature and the Sovereign a participation in the Elective Franchise and the benefit of the Trial by Jury.—It is worthy of remark, that this Letter is utterly silent upon the ground of conſtitutional right, and never ſtates this application as intended to be made upon any other principle than as a neceſſary means of ſecuring to the Catholics an equal acceſs to Leaſehold Property and a fair Diſtribution of Juſtice.—Upon this proceeding, ſo ſimple, and ſo obviouſly conformable to the fundamental principles of Law and Conſtitution, Pettifogging Chicane, ſitting in council with Bigotry and Nonſenſe, having *ingeniouſly* diſcovered that the Letter was circulated with great ſecrecy, pronounces the publication to be of a moſt dangerous, ſeditious, and inflammatory tendency—the phantom of a Popiſh Congreſs is raiſed—the ſcare-crow image of a French National Aſſembly is conjured up—the viſion of a Gun-powder plot appears—and the ſuppliant Committee of an enſlaved people is identified with Sovereign Legiſlative Bodies.

We ſay " enſlaved", for it will not be denied that a people are enſlaved, who being excluded from all ſhare in the Legiſlature of their country, are nevertheleſs ſubject to Laws and Taxes impoſed on them without their conſent.—" Law to bind all muſt be aſſented to by all."—It is not in a ſyſtem of extirpation by penal laws—it is in the free agency of the people that we are to ſeek for the true and permanent principle of a free and proſperous government.—The man who ſays that a political conſtitution can be upheld by penal laws, may ſay that the human conſtitution can be nouriſhed by the uſe of ſlow poiſon.

Where ſo ſmall a portion of ſo large a maſs exerciſes the Elective Franchiſe, and a decided majority of that ſmall portion forms the notorious property of a venal Ariſtocracy, we conſider the Elective Body of the people as nothing more than the ſemblance of a larger Species of Corporation.—Hence, that political Ignorance, that ſelfiſh ſpirit of monopoly, that jealous hoſtility to the general happineſs, which muſt ever characteriſe theſe avaricious retailers of freedom, have alſo infected a great number of the Elective Body of the nation.

Hirelings, whom we have at all prices, cry out, THAT THE CATHOLICS PREFER THEIR COMPLAINTS IN A STILE OF DEMAND.—Such language could not have been uttered in a FREE land; it is the inſolent dictation of deſpotiſm; its authors may wiſh for fellow-ſlaves, but we wiſh for fellow-citizens. The Catholics have ever addreſſed the Legiſlature with due reſpect; their ſubmiſſive conduct is unqueſtionable: but in our mind they only ſhew themſelves worthy of their rights, when they reclaim them.

Is it meant to deny them the right of petitioning?—To queſtion their right of meeting peaceably for that purpoſe amounts to ſuch a denial. This would be a falſe as well as a moſt miſchievous doctrine; for it would neceſſarily throw the ſubject upon the alternative of violence.—He muſt either ſuffer or reſiſt;—and of courſe he muſt ſilently ſink under Deſpotiſm or break out into Anarchy.—When the *Innocent* are puniſhed by law, the ſeverity of Negro-ſervitude alone could preclude them from the right of petitioning.

If the charges made againſt the Catholic Committee were founded in truth, Grand Juries, under the obligations of their oath and public ſtation, ſhould have preſented them—if falſe, then have grand Grand Juries been guilty of defamatory libels.

What ſecurity do we require of our Catholic brethren?—Political miſtruſt has not yet deviſed a teſt, which they have not cheerfully taken. They diſclaim all thoſe abominable principles inconſiſtent with good government which have been falſely imputed to them by thoſe whoſe monopoly was ſuſtained by the diviſions of their country. They avow their ſupport of the church eſtabliſhment. They are even willing to worſhip that new born Chimera, "The Proteſtant Aſcendency," provided the jealous Idol may be appeaſed without the ſacrifice of the Elective Franchiſe and the Trial by Jury. Popery is no longer to be met with, but in the ſtatute book. The Catholics ſtand before us as POLITICAL PROTESTANTS, for they proteſt againſt the errors of the State, and endeavour to eſtabliſh the REFORMATION of the Conſtitution.

Will the men who ſuborn this upſtart zeal for the integrity of the Conſtitution, ſubmit their labours for its preſervation during ſome years paſt to a candid and critical examination?—Short is the catalogue of THEIR ſervices—what has ſignalized their political career? What, but an uniform exertion to ſtifle all efforts for the eſtabliſhment of Iriſh freedom.—Indignant at the odious review, and the treacherous conſiſtency of their preſent conduct, we gladly turn away to acknowledge with pride, that the virtuous founder of the Revolution of 1782 is alſo the leader in the great patriotic work of this day.

As for our part, aſſociated for the attainment of univerſal emancipation and repreſentative Legiſlature, we cannot ſeparate our duty to our country from our duty to our countrymen. The grievances they ſuffer are the grievances of the nation; the relief they ſolicit is the relief of the nation; and as the only true policy of ſtates as well as of individuals is Juſtice, we cheriſh the grateful hope that the riſing ſpirit of Union in a liberal age is the harbinger of its triumph.

Signed by Order,

THOMAS WRIGHT, *Sec.*

UNITED IRISHMEN OF DUBLIN.

The Hon. SIMON BUTLER in the Chair.

THE SOCIETY of UNITED IRISHMEN in DUBLIN. Addreſs the FRIENDS of the PEOPLE at LONDON. Impreſſed with the reſemblance in the title, nature and deſtination of their reſpective inſtitutions; and acting under that fraternity of feeling, which ſuch a co-inſidence naturally inſpires. The title which you bear is a glorious one, and we too are Friends of the People. If we be aſked " who are the People?" we turn not our eyes here and there, to this party, or to that perſuaſion, and cry, " Lo! the people; but we look around us without partiality or predilection, and we anſwer, the multitude of human beings, the living maſs of humanity aſſociated to exiſt, to ſubſiſt, and to be happy. In them and them only we find the original of ſocial authority, the meaſure of political value, and the pedeſtal of legitimate power.

As friends of the People, upholding their rights, and deploring their ſufferings, the great object of this Society is a real repreſentation of the Iriſh Nation in an Iriſh Parliament; and as friends of the whole people, we ſupport the neceſſity of Catholic emancipation as a means of making repreſentation what it ought to be, Free, Equal, and Entire. If the people of one country be not obliged to obey the laws of another, on the ſame principle when the people reſident in a country, have no ſort of influence over the legiſlature, that legiſlature will receive rather a diſcretional acquieſcence than legitimate obedience; and as this diſcretional ſtate is dangerous, becauſe precarious, a change becomes neceſſary for the peace and happineſs of the nation, violence being the laſt meaſure to which rational beings will reſort.

The preſent ſtate of Ireland with regard to Population is upwards of four millions, three of which are of the Catholic Religion; and with regard to Political freedom.

1. The State of *Proteſtant* repreſentation is as follows: 17 Boroughs have no reſident elector; 16 have but one; 16 have from 2 to 5; 90 have 13 electors each; 90 perſons return for 106 venal boroughs, that is 212 members out of 300, the whole number. 54 Members are returned by five noblemen and four biſhops, and borough influence has given landlords ſuch power in the counties as makes them boroughs alſo—53 peers nominates 124 Members, and influence 10, ſo that 228 are returned by 105 Individuals, leaving only 72 out of 300 to the free election of the people. One Lord who nominates 4 Members, is not a Peer of Ireland, and eleven Lords who

are Irish Peers, are absentees, and spend their fortunes out of the realm; to the representation of which they send their commands and are obeyed, notwithstanding two solemn votes of the Commons against this high infringement of their Liberties and Privileges. In short, representation, which in its nature is only a deposit, has been converted into a property, and that constitution which is founded on equal liberty, and which declares that no tax shall be levied without the "good will" of the people, is totally perverted in its principles and corrupted in its practice; yet the majesty of the people is still quoted with affected veneration; and if the crown be ostensibly placed on a part of the Protestant portion, it is placed in mockery, for it is encircled with thorns.

2. With regard to the *Catholics*, the following is the simple and sorrowful fact: Three millions, every one of whom has an interest in the state, and collectively give it its value, are taxed without being represented, and bound by laws to which they have not given consent. They now require a share of political liberty, in the participation of the Elective Franchise, and of civil liberty in the privilege of serving on Grand Juries. There can be no civil without political liberty, and in requiring the right of suffrage they in reality demand only a safeguard for their religion, their property and their lives.

The code of penal Laws against the Catholics reduced oppression into a system: The action and pressure of this system continually accumulating without any re-action on the part of the sufferers, sunk in the lethargy of servitude, have confirmed the governing portion of the people in a habit of domination. This *Habit*, mixing with the antipathies of past times, and the irritations of the moment, has impressed a strange persuasion, that the rights of the plurality are Protestant *property*, and that the birth-right of millions, born and to be born, continue the spoils of war and booty of conquest. The perversion of the understanding perverts the heart, and this Protestant ascendancy, as it calls itself, uniting power with passion, and hating the Catholics because it has injured them, on a bare inquisitorial suspicion, insufficient to criminate an individual, would erase a whole people from the roll of citizenship, and for the sins (if they were sins) of remote ancestors would attaint their remotest posterity. We have read, and read with horror, that Louis 11th, ordered the children to be placed under the scaffold where the father was beheaded, that they might be sprinkled with his blood.

Is it, we think, by this unequal distribution of popular privilege, that its very nature has, in this kingdom, been corrupted, and from the moment that equality of rights was overturned, and general liberty became particular power, the public mind has been split into a conflict of factions. General distribution of the elective franchise would make corruption impracticable, but when common right becomes the property of person, party or persuasion, it acquires a value equally unnatural and unconstitutional; is bought and sold; rises or falls, like any marketable commodity. The *deprivation* of the elective franchise, on the one hand, robs a great majority of the nation of an invaluable blessing; and its *accumulation* in the hands of the Protestant portion, operates on that very portion as a curse. The right of *all*, heaped up and hoarded by the *few*, becomes a public pest, and the nutriment of the constitution is changed into its poison. The iniquitous monopoly rots in boroughs;

ſpreads its contagion through counties; taints morals and manners; makes elections mere fairs for the traffic of franchiſe and the ſale of men; in place of that nationality of mind which ſpreads its parental embrace around a whole people, ſubſtitutes the envious, excluding ſpirit of ſelfiſh corporations; and ſwelling, at length, into monſtrous and gigantic aſcendancy, holds forth a hundred thouſand hands to bribe and betray, and tramples with a hundred thouſand feet on thoſe miſerable millions who have loſt their only guarantee againſt injuſtice and oppreſſion.

Inſtructed by the Genius of the Conſtitution, and the genuine Spirit of the Laws; inſtructed, of late, by all that has been ſpoken, or written, or acted, or ſuffered in the cauſe of freedom; inſtructed by the late revolution in America, by the late revolution in Ireland, by the late revo-in France; hearing of all that has been done over the face of the globe for Liberty, and feeling all that can be ſuffered from the want of it; reading the charter of independence to Ireland, and liſtening to the ſpirit-ſtirring voice of her great deliverer; actuated, in fine, by that imperiſhable ſpark in the boſom of man which the ſervitude of a century may ſmother, but cannot extinguiſh, the Catholics of this country have been leſſoned into liberty, have learned to know their rights, to be ſenſible of their wrongs, and to detail by peaceable delegation, their grievances, rather than endure without obedience. You!—in either kingdoms, who reproach the Catholics of Ireland for aſſerting the rights of nature, burn your books, tear your charters, break down your free preſs, and crumble to pieces thoſe moulds which have caſt liberty in ſo fair a form, as to make Catholics feel what Proteſtants have felt, and join their admiration and love with thoſe of a worſhipping world.

This Society and many other Societies have aſſociated to create that union of power, and that brotherhood of affection among all the inhabitants of this Iſland, which is the intereſt as well as duty of all. We are all Iriſhmen, and our object is to unite the different deſcriptions of religion in the cauſe of our common country. From the moſt oppoſite points in the wide circumference of religions we tend with increaſing velocity to the ſame centre of political union. A reform in parliament preceding Catholic enfranchiſement would be in its nature partial and excluſive, and unleſs a reform immediately follows that emancipation (which it will certainly do) the extenſion of elective franchiſe, would only add to the maſs of corruption. The centre of our union is fixed and immoveable. The Preſbyterian wiſhes for national freedom. The Catholic aſpires to nothing more; nor can either of them be brought to believe that thoſe varieties of religious faith, which may be deemed the pleaſures of the Creator, ſhould be made the engines of political torture to any of his creatures. Too long have our people been ſet in array of battle againſt each other; too long have the rancour and revenge of our anceſtors been left as a legacy of blood to their poſterity; too long has one limb of the ſocial body been tied down, until it had nearly loſt all feeling, life and energy. It is our wiſh, it is our hope, to give Ireland the full and free poſſeſſion of both her arms, her Catholic arm as well as her Proteſtant arm, that ſhe may the better embrace her Friends or grapple with her Foes.

Such are the principles and practice of our Inſtitution, which having neither power nor patronage, but merely the energy of honeſty, has not only been diſtinguiſhed by the calumnies of thoſe who are born only to bite the heel, and be cruſhed under foot, but has been honoured by the obloquy of men who fill the firſt offices in the ſtate. From them we appeal to natural right, and eternal juſtice, which ought ever to be eſtabliſhed without compromiſe or reſervation. From them we appeal to thoſe who call themſelves Friends of the People. Look not upon Ireland with an eye of indifference. The period of Iriſh inſignificance is paſſing faſt away. If the nation ever appeared contemptible, it was becauſe the nation did not act; but no ſooner in the late war was it abandoned by Government, than it roſe to diſtinction as a People. As to any union between the iſlands, believe us when we aſſert that our union reſts upon our mutual independence. We ſhall love each other, *if we be left to ourſelves*. It is the union of *minds* which ought to bind theſe nations together. Reciprocal intereſts and mutual wants will ever ſecure mutual affection; but were any other union to be forced, and force only could effect it, you would endanger your liberties, and we ſhould loſe our rights; you would feel the influence of the crown increaſe beyond all ſufferance, and we ſhould loſe the name and energies of a people, with every hope of raiſing to its merited ſtation in the map of mankind this noble and neglected Iſland " for which God has done ſo much and Man ſo little."

Signed by Order,

THOMAS WRIGHT, *Secretary.*

Dublin, October 26th, 1792.

November 3, 1792.

To WILLIAM DRENNAN, M. D.
Chairman.

OF THE SOCIETY OF UNITED IRISHMEN

IN DUBLIN.

SIR,

AS Chairman of the Catholics of Dublin, I am ordered to transmit a copy of their proceedings on Wednesday, October 31st.

We trust you will find in that paper, a just reflection of your own principles, no less honourable to yourselves, than advantageous to the true interests of your Country.

With every sentiment of gratitude for the services which the Catholic cause has received at your hands, we are Sir, your most obliged and obedient servants,

By order of the Meeting,

THOMAS BRAUGHAL, *Chairman.*

October 31, 1792.

CATHOLIC MEETING OF DUBLIN.

RESOLVED

THAT we embrace this opportunity to repeat our Thanks to the illuſtrious Characters in both Houſes of Parliament, who have nobly ſtood forward in ſupport of Catholic Emancipation, and the Right of the Subject to Petition for Redreſs of Grievances.

That our warmeſt Gratitude is due and hereby reſpectfully offered to our countrymen, the Citizens of Belfaſt, for the uniform and manly exertions which they have on all occaſions made in ſupport of our cauſe, and for the example of liberality and genuine public ſpirit which they have thereby ſhewn to the kingdom at large.

That our ſincere Thanks are likewiſe due to the different Volunteer Corps lately reviewed in Ulſter, to the Societies of United Iriſhmen of Dublin and Belfaſt, to the Proteſtant Freeholders of Cork, the different Gentlemen who at Grand Juries and County Meetings have ſupported our Cauſe, and to all others among our Proteſtant Brethren, who have manifeſted a wiſh for our Emancipation; and we truſt we ſhall evince by our conduct, that we are not inſenſible nor unworthy of the kindneſs which they have ſhewn us.

That our Chairman be ordered to tranſmit Copies of this Day's proceedings to the Chairman of the Town-Meeting of Belfaſt, the Chairman of the different Societies of United Iriſhmen, the different Reviewing Officers in Ulſter, and the other diſtinguiſhed Characters who have intereſt themſelves in the Cauſe of Catholic Emancipation.

By Order of the Meeting

SIMON Mc. GUIRE, *Secretary*.

November 23, 1792.

ADDRESS FROM THE SOCIETY OF UNITED IRISHEN IN DUBLIN, TO THE DELEGATES FOR PROMOTING A REFORM IN SCOTLAND.

WILLIAM DRENNAN, *Chairman*.

ARCHIBALD HAMILTON ROWAN, *Sec*.

WE take the liberty of addreſſing you, in the ſpirit of civil union, in the fellowſhip of a juſt and a common cauſe. We greatly rejoice that the ſpirit of freedom moves over the face of Scotland; that light ſeems to break from the chaos of her internal government; and that a country ſo reſpectable for her attainments in ſcience, in arts, and in arms; for men of literary eminence; for the intelligence and morality of her people, now acts from a conviction of the union between virtue, letters, and liberty: and, now riſes to diſtinction, not by a calm, contented, ſecret wiſh for a Reform in Parliament, but by openly, actively, and urgently *willing* it, with the unity and energy of an embodied nation. We rejoice that you do not confider yourfelves as merged and melted down into another country, but that in this great national queftion, you are ftill—Scotland—the land where Buchanan wrote, and Fletcher fpoke, and Wallace fought.

Away from us and from our children thofe puerile antipathies fo unworthy of the manhood of nations, which infulate individuals as well as countries, and drive the citizen back to the favage. We efteem and we refpect you. We pay merited honour to a nation in general well educated, and well informed, becaufe we know that the ignorance of the people is the caufe and effect of all civil and religious defpotifm. We honour a nation regular in their lives, and ftrict in their manners, becaufe we conceive private morality to be the only fecure foundation of public policy. We honour a nation eminent for men of genius, and we truft that they will now exert themfelves not fo much in perufing and penning the hiftories of other countries, as in making their own a fubject for the hiftorian. May we venture to obferve to them that mankind have been too retrofpective; canonized antiquity, and undervalued themfelves. Man has repofed on ruins, and refted his head on fome fragments of the temple of liberty, or at moft amufed himfelf in pacing the meafurement of the edifice, and nicely limiting its proportions; not reflecting that this temple is truly Catholic, the ample earth its area, and the arch of heaven, its dome.

We will lay open to you our hearts. Our caufe is your caufe—If there is to be a ftruggle between us, let it be which nation fhall be foremoft in the race of mind: let this be the noble animofity kindled between us, who fhall firft attain that free conftitution from which both are equidiftant, who fhall firft be the faviour of the empire.

The ſenſe of both countries with reſpect to the intolerable abuſes of the conſtitution has been clearly manifeſted, and proves that our political ſituations are not diſſimilar; that our rights and wrongs are the ſame. Out of 32 counties in Ireland, 29 petitioned for a Reform in Parliament: and out of 56 of the royal Burghs in Scotland, 50 petitioned for a Reform in their internal ſtructure and Government. If we be rightly informed, there is no ſuch thing as popular election in Scotland. The people who ought to poſſeſs that weight in the political ſcale, which might bind them to the ſoil, and make them cling to the conſtitution, are now as duſt in the ballance, blown abroad by the leaſt impulſe, and ſcattered through other countries, merely becauſe they hang ſo looſely to their own. They have no ſhare in the national *Firm*, and are aggrieved not only by irregular and illegal exaction of taxes; by miſrule and miſmanagement of corporations; by miſconduct of ſelf-elected and irreſponſible magiſtrates; by waſte of public property; and by want of competent judicatures; but, in our opinion, moſt of all, by an inadequate Parliamentary repreſentation —for, we aſſert, that 45 Commoners and 16 Peers, are a pitiful repreſentation for two millions, and a half of people; particularly as your Commoners conſider themſelves not as the repreſentatives of that people, but of the Councils of the Burghs by whom they are elected.

Excluſive charters in favour of Boroughs, monopolize the general rights of the people, and that act muſt be abſurd which precludes all other towns from the power of being reſtored to their ancient freedom.

We remember that heretable juriſdictions and feudal privileges, though expreſſly reſerved by the act of union (20th art.) were ſet aſide by Act of

Parliament in 1746, and we think that there is much ſtronger ground at preſent, for reſtoring to the maſs of the people, their alienated rights, and to the Conſtitution its ſpirit and its integrity.

Look now we pray you upon IRELAND. Long was this unfortunate Iſland the prey of prejudiced factions and ferocious parties. The rights or rather duties of conqueſt were dreadfully abuſed, and the Catholic religion was made the perpetual pretext for ſubjecting the ſtate by annihilating the citizen, and deſtroying not the religious perſuaſion but the man; not popery, but the people. It was not till very lately that the part of the nation which is truly colonial, reflected that though their anceſtors had been victorious, they themſelves were now included in the general ſubjection; ſubduing only to be ſubdued, and trampled upon by Britain as a ſervile dependency. When therefore the Proteſtants began to ſuffer what the Catholics had ſuffered and were ſuffering; when from ſerving as the inſtruments they were made themſelves the objects of foreign domination, then they became conſcious they had a country: and then they felt—an Ireland. They reſiſted Britiſh dominion, renounced colonial ſubſerviency, and following the example of a Catholic Parliament juſt a century before, they aſſerted the excluſive juriſdiction and legiſlative competency of this Iſland. A ſudden light from America ſhone through our priſon. Our Volunteers aroſe. The chains fell from our hands. We followed Grattan, the angel of our deliverance, and in 1782 Ireland ceaſed to be a province and became a nation. But, with reaſon, ſhould we deſpiſe and renounce this Revolution as merely a tranſient burſt through a bad habit; the ſudden graſp of neceſſity in deſpair, from tyranny in diſtreſs, did we not believe that the Revolution is ſtill *in train*; that it is leſs the ſingle and ſhining act of 82, than a ſeries of national improvements which that act uſhers in and announces; that it is only the herald of liberty and glory, of Catholic emancipation, as well as Proteſtant independence; that, in ſhort, this Revolution indicates new principles, foreruns new practice, and lays a foundation for advancing the whole people higher in the ſcale of being, and diffuſing equal and permanent happineſs.

Britiſh ſupremacy changed its aſpect, but its eſſence remained the ſame. Firſt it was force,* and on the event of the late Revolution, it became influence; direct hoſtility ſhifted into ſyſtematic corruption, ſilently drawing off the virtue and vigour of the iſland, without ſhock or exploſion.—Corruption that glides into every place, tempts every perſon, taints every principle, infects the political mind through all its relations and dependencies; ſo regardleſs of public character as to ſet the higheſt honours to ſale, and to purchaſe Boroughs with the price of ſuch proſtitution; ſo regardleſs of private morality, as to legalize the licentiouſneſs of the loweſt and moſt pernicious gambling, and to extract a calamitous revenue from the infatuation and intoxication of the people.

The Proteſtants of Ireland were now ſenſible that nothing could counteract this plan of debilitating policy, but a radical reform in the Houſe of the People, and that without ſuch reform, the Revolution itſelf was nominal and deluſive. The wheel merely turned round, but it did not move forward, and they were as diſtant as ever from the gaol. They reſolved.—They convened—They met with arms.—They met without them.—They petitioned. But all in vain—for, they were but a portion of the people. Then they looked around and beheld their Catholic countrymen. Three million—we repeat it—three million taxed without being repreſented, bound by laws to which they had not given conſent, and politically dead in their native land. The apathy of the Catholic mind changed into ſympathy, and that begot an energy of ſentiment and action. They had eyes, and they read. They had ears and they liſtened. They had hearts, and they felt. They ſaid—"Give us our rights as you value your own. Give us a ſhare of civil and political liberty, the elective franchiſe, and the trial by jury. Treat us as men and we ſhall treat you as brothers. Is taxation without repreſentation a grievance to three millions acroſs the Atlantic, and no grievance to three millions at your doors? Throw down that pale of perſecution which ſtill keeps up civil war in Ireland, and make us one people. We ſhall then ſtand, ſupporting and ſupported, in the aſſertion of that liberty which is due to all, and which all ſhould unite to attain."

It was juſt—and immediately a principle of adheſion took place for the firſt time, among the inhabitants of Ireland. All religious perſuaſions found in a political union their common duty and their common ſalvation. In this SOCIETY and its affiliated Societies, the Catholic and the Preſbyterian are at this inſtant holding out their hands and opening their hearts to each other, agreeing in principles, concurring in practice. We unite for immediate, ample, and ſubſtantial juſtice to the Catholics, and when that is attained, a combined exertion for a reform in Parliament is the condition of our compact, and the ſeal of our communion.

Britiſh ſupremacy takes alarm. The haughty monopoliſts of national power and common right, who crouch abroad, to domineer at home, now look with more ſurpriſe and leſs contempt on this "besotted" people. A new artifice is adopted, and that restless domination which, at first, ruled as open war, by the length of the sword; then, as covert corruption, by the strength of the poison; now assumes the stile and title of Protestant Ascendancy; calls down the name of religion from heaven to sow discord on earth; to rule by anarchy; to keep up distrust and antipathy among parties, among persuasions, among families, nay to make the passions of the individuals struggle, like Cain and Abel, in the very home of the heart, and to convert every little paltry necessity that accident, indolence, or extravagance, bring upon a man, into a pandar for the purchase of his honesty and the murder of his reputation.

We will not be the dupes of such ignoble artifices. We see this scheme of strengthening political persecution and state inquisition, by a fresh infusion of religious fanaticism—but we will unite and we will be Free. *Universal Emancipation with Representative Legislature* is the polar principle which guides our Society and shall guide it through all the tumult of factions and fluctuations of parties. It is not upon a coalition of opposition with ministry that we depend, but upon a coalition of Irishmen with Irishmen, and in that coalition alone we find an object worthy of reform, and at the same time the strength and sinew both to attain and secure it. It is not upon external circumstances, upon the pledge of man or minister, we depend, but upon the internal energy of the Irish Nation. We will not buy or borrow liberty from America or from France, but manufacture it ourselves, and work it up with those materials which the hearts of Irishmen furnish them with at home. We do not worship the British, far less the Irish Constitution, as sent down from heaven, but we consider it as human workmanship, which man has made and man can mend. An inalterable Conſtitution, whatever be its naure, muſt be deſpotiſm. It is not the conſtitution but the People which ought to be inviolable, and it is time to recognize and renovate the rights of the Engliſh, the Scotch, and the Iriſh Nations.—Rights which can neither be bought nor ſold, granted by charter, or foreſtalled by monopoly, but which nature dictates as the birth-right of all, and which it is the buſineſs of a Conſtitution to define, to enforce, and to eſtabliſh. If Government has a ſincere regard for the ſafety of the conſtitution, let them coincide with the people in the ſpeedy reform of its abuſes, and not by an obſtinate adherence to them, drive that people into Republicaniſm

We have told you what our ſituation was, what it is, what it ought to be: our end, a National Legiſlature; our means, an union of the whole people. Let this union extend throughout the Empire. Let all unite for all, or each man ſuffer for all. In each country let the people aſſemble in peaceful and conſtitutional Convention. Let delegates from each country digeſt a plan of reform, beſt adapted to the ſituation and circumſtances of their reſpective nations, and let the Legiſlatures be petitioned at once by the urgent and unanimous voice of England, Scotland, and Ireland.

You have our ideas. Anſwer us, and that quickly. This is not a time to procraſtinate. Your illuſtrious Fletcher has ſaid, that the liberties of a people are not to be ſecured, without paſſing through great difficulties, and no toil or labours ought to be declined to preſerve a nation from ſlavery. He ſpoke well: and we add, that it is incumbent on every nation who adventures into a conflict for freedom, to remember it is on the event (however abſurdly) depends the eſtimation of public opinion; honour and immortality, if fortunate; if otherwise, infamy and oblivion. Let this check the rashness that rushes unadvisedly into the committal of national character, or *if that be already made*, let the same consideration impel us all to advance with active not passive perseverance, with manly confidence and calm determination, smiling with equal scorn at the bluster of official arrogance, and the whisper of private malevolence, until we have planted the flag of Freedom on the summit, and are at once victorious and secure.

November 30, 1792.

UNITED IRISHMEN OF DUBLIN,

WILLIAM DRENNAN in the Chair.

TO THE CHAIRMAN OF THE SOCIETY OF

UNITED IRISHMEN OF

(Circular,)

SIR,

THIS Society has passed a resolution, " that we do proceed immediately to effect a better organiation and a more intimate union with the different Societies of United Irishmen than has hitherto subsisted. We are also enjoined by a subsequent order to communicate all the publications of this Body to the Confederated Societies. We shall accordingly now and henceforward transmit to you all such papers and we solicit the satisfaction of your concurrence to carry these resolutions into effect.

Our general principles and motives of aſſociation are amply detailed in our circular letter and declaration: but as our objects are of the firſt moment in life, the particular conduct of thoſe Societies who co-operate with us, is of correſpondent importance. It appears to us, at this intereſting criſis, incumbent on patriotic aſſociations of virtuous and independent men to eſtabliſh frequent meetings, and a mutual communication of all their proceedings. Well aſſured that a fund of good ſenſe and patriotiſm ſtill exiſts latent among us, it is our common duty to call forth this valuable maſs into life. Silence now becomes criminal, and neutrality treaſonable. The private advocate of Catholic emancipation and repreſentative legiſlature will be reckoned among our Enemies, and employed as the paſſive inſtrument of their artifices. We ſhould therefore hold a ſtrict inqueſt of all public meaſures, labour to give uniſon to the public ſentiment, and fix its ſtandard. It becomes us to interfere, when Grand Juries follow the example of the Houſe of Commons and miſrepreſent the People. We muſt not ſuffer Falſehood to ſtalk over the Land in Right Honourable Solemnity, to invade the National Credit, and arraign the National Character—we muſt arreſt its progreſs, and arraign its Authors at the Bar of the Nation..

We cannot too ſtrongly impreſs upon the public mind, that the repeal of this or that obnoxious Law out of the multitude,—that the removal from power of this or that party, can only ſhift our poſition upon the Wheel of Political Torture. Parties have changed, and Palliatives have been adminiſtered; but the Traffic of Iriſh Freedom, and the Plunder of Iriſh Property have been uniform and permanent. It becomes therefore our eſſential duty to direct the Eye of the People to the Polar Star of their political ſalvation, a Repreſentative Legiſlature, while the Echo of that *Watch-word* of *Diſcord*, that *Motto* of *Proſtitution*, the Proteſtant Aſcendancy, dies away through reptile Corporations.

Finally, in reliance that you have adopted the Letter of our Teſt, we recommend it to your zeal to diffuſe its Spirit; becauſe it engrafts the firſt duty of a good Citizen upon the firſt duty of a good Chriſtian; becauſe it is a practice ſubverſive of our Conſtitution, that the King and the Lords ſhould vote in the Commons Houſe of Parliament, that the Maſs of the People ſhould be excluded from their inalienable Share in the Legiſlature, not by the inſenſible abuſes of time, but by an expreſs Law; and becauſe this excluſion eſtabliſhes, under the maſk of Freedom, a Syſtem of Practical Deſpotiſm over the whole People.

Preſcribing theſe Duties to ourſelves, we ſubmit them to your conſideration, and requeſt the favour of your correſpondence.

I am, Sir, with great Reſpect,
Your obedient humble Servant,
A. HAMILTON ROWAN, Secretary.

December 7, 1792.

RESOLVED,

THAT having ſo frequently avowed our ſentiments on Univerſal Emancipation, and Repreſentative Legiſlature, it is not neceſſary for us at this time to repeat that the Delegates of the Catholic People in the faithful diſcharge of their ſacred truſt, as tending to the Eſtabliſhment of perfect Freedom in the Nation, may be aſſured of our zealous co-operation.

December 14, 1792.

THE SOCIETY OF UNITED IRISHMEN,

AT DUBLIN, TO THE VOLUNTEERS.

OF IRELAND,

WILLIAM DRENNAN, *Chairman*.

ARCHIBALD HAMILTON ROWAN, *Sec*.

CITIZEN SOLDIERS,

YOU firſt took up arms to protect your Country from foreign enemies, and from domeſtic diſturbance. For the ſame purpoſes, it now becomes neceſſary that you ſhould reſume them. A Proclamation has been iſſued in England for embodying the Militia, and a Proclamation has been iſſued by the Lord Lieutenant and Council in Ireland, for repreſſing all *ſeditious* aſſociations. In conſequence of both theſe Proclamations, it is reaſonable to apprehend danger from abroad, and danger at home. For whence but from apprehended danger are thoſe menacing preparations for war drawn through the Streets of this Capital, or whence, if not to *create* that internal commotion which was not *found*, to ſhake that credit which was not *affected*, to blaſt that Volunteer honour which was hitherto *inviolate*, are thoſe terrible ſuggeſtions and rumours and whiſpers, that meet us at every corner and agitate at leaſt our old men, our women and children. Whatever be the motive, or from whatever quarter it ariſes, alarm has ariſen; and you, VOLUNTEERS OF IRELAND, are therefore ſummoned *To Arms* at the inſtance of Government, as well as by the reſponſibility attached to your character, and the permanent obligations of your institution. We will not at this day, condescend to quote authorities for the *right* of having and of using arms, but we will cry aloud, even amidst the storm raised by the Witchcraft of a proclamation, That to your *formation* was owing the peace and protection of this Island, to your *relaxation* has been owing its relapse into impotence and insignificance, to your *renovation* must be owing its future freedom and its present tranquillity. You are therefore summoned to Arms, in order to preserve your country in that guarded quiet, which may secure it from external hostility, and to maintain that internal regimen throughout the land, which superseding a notorious Police or a suspected Militia, may preserve the blessings of peace by a vigilant preparation for war.

Citizen Soldiers, to arms! Take up the shield of Freedom, and the pledges of Peace,—Peace, the motive and end of your virtuous institution.—War, an occasional duty, ought never to be made an occupation. Every man should become a Soldier in the defence of his rights; no man ought to continue a soldier for offending the rights of others. The sacrifice of life in the service of our country is a duty much too honourable to be intrusted to mercenaries, and at this time, when your country has by public authority been declared in danger, we conjure you by your interest, your duty and your glory, to stand to your arms, and in spite of a Police, in spite of a Fencible Militia, in virtue of two Proclamations, to maintain good order in your vicinage and tranquility in Ireland.—It is only by the military array of men in whom they confide, whom they have been accustomed to revere as the guardians of domestic peace, the protectors of their liberties and lives, that the present agitation of the people can be ſtilled, that tumult and licentiouſneſs can be repreſſed, obedience ſecured to exiſting law, and a calm confidence, diffuſed through the public mind in the ſpeedy reſurrection of a free conſtitution—of *Liberty* and of *Equality*,—words which we uſe for an opportunity of repelling calumny and of ſaying, that,

By Liberty we never underſtood unlimited freedom, nor by Equality the levelling of property, or the deſtruction of ſubordination.—This is a calumny invented by that faction or that gang which miſrepreſents the King to the People, and the People to the King, traduces one half of the nation to cajole the other, and by keeping up diſtruſt and diviſion, wiſhes to continue the proud arbitrators of the fortune and fate of Ireland.—Liberty is the exerciſe of all our rights natural and political, ſecured to us and our poſterity by a real repreſentation of the people ;—and equality is the extenſion of the conſtituent, to the fulleſt dimenſions of the conſtitution, of the elective franchiſe to the whole body of the people, to the end that government which is collective power, may be guided by collective will, and that legiſlation may originate from public reaſon, keep peace with public improvement, and terminate in public happineſs. If our conſtitution be imperfect, nothing but a reform in repreſentation will rectify its abuſes ; if it be perfect, nothing but the ſame Reform will perpetuate its bleſſings.

We now addreſs you as Citizens, for to be Citizens you became Soldiers, nor can we help wiſhing that all Soldiers, partaking the paſſions, and intereſt of the people would remember that they were once Citizens, that ſeduction made them Soldiers,—" but nature made them Men." We addreſs you without any authority ſave that of reaſon, and if we obtain the coincidence of public opinion it is neither by force nor ſtratagem, for we have no power to terrify, no artifice to cajole, no fund to ſeduce.—Here we ſit,—without mace or beadle, neither a myſtery nor a craft, nor a Corporation.——In four words lies all our Power, UNIVERSAL EMANCIPATION and REPRESENTATIVE LEGISLATURE; yet we are confident that on the pivot of this principle, a convention,—ſtill leſs,—a ſociety,—leſs ſtill,—a ſingle man, will be able, firſt to move and then to raiſe the world. We, therefore, wiſh for Catholic emancipation without any modification, but ſtill we conſider this neceſſary enfranchiſement as merely the portal to the Temple of National Freedom. Wide as this entrance is, wide enough to admit three millions,—it is narrow, when compared to the capacity and comprehenſion of our beloved principle, which takes in every individual of the Iriſh nation, caſts an equal eye over the whole Iſland, embraces all that think and feels for all that ſuffer. The Catholic cauſe is ſubordinate to our cauſe, and included in it, for as UNITED IRISHMEN, we adhere to no ſect, but to ſociety, to no creed but Chriſtianity, to no party, but the whole people.—In the ſincerity of our ſouls, do we deſire Catholic emancipation, but were it obtained, to-morrow, to-morrow would we go on, as we do to-day, in the purſuit of that reform which would ſtill be wanting to ratify their liberties as well as our own.

For both theſe purpoſes, it appears neceſſary that provincial conventions ſhould aſſemble preparatory to the convention of the Proteſtant People. The Delegates of the Catholic body are not juſtified in communicating with individuals, or even bodies of inferior authority, and therefore an Aſſembly of a ſimilar nature and organization is neceſſary to eſtabliſh an intercourſe of ſentiment, anuniformity of conduct, an united cause, and an united nation. If a convention on the one part does not soon follow, and is not soon connected with that on the other, the common cause will split into the partial interest; the people will relax into inattention and inertness; the union of affection and exertion will dissolve, and too probably some local insurrection, instigated by the malignity of our common enemy, may commit the character, and risque the tranquillity of the Island, which can be obviated only by the influence of an assembly arising from, assimilated with the people, and whose spirit may be as it were knit with the soul of the nation,—unless the sense of the Protestant People, be, on their part, as fairly collected and as judiciously directed, unless individual exertion consolidates into collective strength, unless the particles unite into mass, we may perhaps serve some person, or some party for a little, but the public not at all. The nation is neither insolent nor rebellious nor seditious. While it knows its rights it is unwilling to manifest its powers. It would rather supplicate administration to anticipate revolution by a well timed reform, and to save their country in mercy to themselves.

The 15th of February approaches, a day ever memorable in the annals of this country as the birth-day of new Ireland—Let parochial meetings be held as soon as possible. Let each Parish return delegates. Let the sense of Ulster be again declared from Dungannon on a day auspicious to union, peace and freedom, and the spirit of the North will again become the spirit of the Nation. The civil assembly ought to claim the attendance of the military associations and we have addressed you, Citizen Soldiers—on this subject, from the belief that your body, uniting conviction with zeal and zeal with activity, may have much influence over your countrymen, your relations and friends. We offer only a general outline to the public, and meaning to addreſs Ireland, we preſume not at preſent to fill up the plan or pre-occupy the mode of its execution. We have thought it our duty to ſpeak: anſwer us by actions; you have taken time for conſideration. Fourteen long years are elapſed ſince the riſe of your aſſociations and in 1782, did you imagine that in 1792 this nation would ſtill remain unrepreſented? How many Nations in this interval have gotten the ſtart of Ireland! How many of our Countrymen have ſunk into the Grave!

December 23, 1792.

UNITED IRISHMEN OF DUBLIN.

WILLIAM DRENNAN, *Chairman.*

ARCHIBALD HAMILTON ROWAN, *Sec.*

RESOLVED, That it appears to this Society, from the Evidence laid before it, that the printed Hand Bills which Archibald Hamilton Rowan and James Napper Tandy are charged, in the Information ſworn againſt them, with having diſtributed, are Copies of the Addreſs of this Society to the Volunteers of Ireland, falſely called in the ſaid Information " A ſeditious Libel."

Reſolved, That it is the Duty of every Member to diſtribute the public Reſolutions of the Society, and if A. H. Rowan and J. N. Tandy really diſtributed that Addreſs, they, in ſo doing, acted agreeable to the Sentiments, and, therefore, merit the Approbation of this Society.

Reſolved, That this Society, in ſupporting its Rights, will not confine itſelf merely to defenſive Meaſures, but as the Sale of the Peerage, and of Seats in the repreſentative Houſe of Parliament, and other Corruptions are openly and notoriouſly practiſed by a ſhameleſs and profligate Adminiſtration, this Society will, without Delay, prepare Materials for Proſecutions againſt ſuch Members of the Adminiſtration as have been guilty of ſuch Enormities.

Reſolved, That although we deſpiſe the paltry Trick by which thoſe, intereſted in the preſent unconſtitutional Repreſentation of the People, endeavour to fix, as a Stigma, the Character of Republican and Leveller on every active Promoter of Reform,—yet, as we ſee with Concern, that ſome well-intentioned and ſincere Friends of that Meaſure have been affected with a Fear artfully and groundleſſly excited for corrupt Purpoſes, we think it our Duty to declare, on our own behalf, that the Object of our Inſtitution is an impartial and adequate Repreſentation of the Iriſh Nation in Parliament;—and, in order to prove, that our Views are, and always have been, directed to that End, we hereunto ſubjoin the Teſt, which was adopted on the Eſtabliſhment of this Society, and which has been uniformly taken by every Member on his admiſſion.

(Note—*See Teſt, page* 5)

Back-lane, January 11th, 1793.

WILLIAM DRENNAN, Chairman,

ARCHIBALD HAMILTON ROWAN, Sec.

THE SOCIETY OF UNITED IRISHMEN

OF THE CITY OF DUBLIN.

UNCONNECTED with Party, faithfully attached to the principles of the Conſtitution, and aſſociated for the attainment of a communion of Rights, and of an equal and impartial Repreſentation of the Nation in Ireland, are happy in expreſſing their tribute of praiſe and gratitude, to their moſt Gracious Sovereign for that part of the Speech from the Throne, whereby his Majeſty particularly recommended to his Parliament, to take into their ſerious conſideration, the ſituation of his Catholic Subjects.

January 25, 1793.

THE SOCIETY OF UNITED IRISHMEN OF DUBLIN.

TO THE IRISH NATION.

WILLIAM DRENNAN, Chairman.

ARCHIBALD HAMILTON ROWAN, Sec.

IT is our right and our duty, at this time and at all times, to communicate our opinion to the public, whatever may be its ſucceſs; and under the protection of a free-preſs, itſelf protected by a jury, judges of law as well as fact, we will never be afraid to ſpeak freely what we freely think, appealing for the purity of our intentions to God, and as far as theſe intentions are manifeſted by word, writing, or action, appealing to the juſtice of our cauſe, and the judgment of our country.

On the 9th of November, 1791, was this Society founded. We and our beloved brethren of Belfaſt firſt began that civic union, which, if a nation be a ſociety united for mutual advantage, has made Ireland a nation; and at a time when all wiſhed, many willed, but few ſpoke, and fewer acted, we, Catholics and Proteſtants, joined our hands and our hearts together; ſunk every diſtinctive appellation in the name *Iriſhman*; and in the preſence of God, devoted ourſelves to univerſal enfranchiſement, and a real repreſentation of all the people in Parliament. On this rock of right our little ark found a reſting-place; gradually, though not ſlowly, throughout the country, other ſtations of ſafety appeared, and what before was agitated ſea, became firm and fertile land. From that time have the body and ſpirit of our Societies increaſed, until ſelfiſh Corporations, ſunk in conſcious inſignificance, have given way to a grand incorporation of the Iriſh People.

We have, in our *Digeſt of the penal laws*, addreſſed ourſelves ſucceſsfully, to the good ſenſe, humanity, and generous indignation of all Ireland, convincing public reaſon, alarming public conſcience, and holding up this collection of bloody fragments as a terrible memorial of government without juſtice, and of legality without conſtitution. It has been our rule and our practice never to enter into compromiſe or compoſition with a noxious principle, and we have therefore ſet our face, and lifted our voice, againſt this perſecuting and puſillanimous code, as againſt the murderer of our brother, eager to eraſe the whole of it from the ſtatute-book as it eraſed our countrymen from the ſtate, and wiſhing to proſcribe ſuch an incongruous and monſtrous conjunction of terms as *Penal Laws* not only from a digeſt of the laws but from the dictionary of the language.

It has appeared our duty, in times ſuch as theſe, when the head is nothing without the heart, and with men ſuch as we oppoſe, not only to write and ſpeak but to act and ſuffer; to reckon nothing hazardous, provided it was neceſſary; to come forward with the intrepidity which a good cauſe inſpires, and a backward people required; by going far ourſelves to make others follow faſter, though, all the time conjuring us to retreat; in ſhort, to make the retrograde ſtationary, and the ſtationary progreſſive;

to quicken the dead, and add a ſoul to the living.

Knowing that what the tongue is to the man, the preſs is to the people, though nearly blaſted in our cradle by the ſorcery of ſolicitors of law, and general attorneys, we have perſiſted with courageous perſeverance to rally around this forlorn hope of freedom, and to maintain this citadel of the conſtitution, at the riſque of perſonal ſecurity, property, and all that was dear to us. They have come to us, with a writ and a warrant, and an ex officio information, but we have come to them in the name of the genius of the Britiſh conſtitution and the majeſty of the people of Ireland. Is ſedition againſt the officers of adminiſtration, to exerciſe the criminal juriſdiction of the country, and is ſedition againſt the people, to walk by with arrogant impunity?

We have defended the violated liberty of the ſubject againſt the undefined and voracious privilege of the Houſe of Commons, treating with merited ſcorn the inſolent menaces of men inflated with office, and not only have we maintained the rights of the people at the bar of this branch of the legiſlature, but we have, at the bench of judicature, vindicated the right of the nation, its real independence and ſupremacy; demonſtrating that general inviolability was made tranſmiſſible to one or many deputies, to the utter extinction of reſponſibility, the evaſion of criminality; and that the executive power of imperial and independent Ireland, was merely a jingling appendage to the great Seal of Great Britain. Not a man ſo low, that, if oppreſſed by an aſſumption of power, civil or military, has not met with our counſel, our purſe and our protection: not a man ſo high, that if acting contrary to popular right or public independence, we have not denounced at the judgment ſeat of juſtice, and at the equitable tribunal of public opinion.

We have encountered much calumny. We have, among a thouſand contradictory epithets been called republicans and levellers, as if by artfully making the terms appear ſynonymous, their nature could be made the ſame; as if a republican were a leveller, or a leveller a republican; as if the only leveller was not the deſpot who cruſhes with an iron ſceptre every rank and degree of ſociety into one; as if republican or democratic energy was not, as well as ariſtocratical privilege, or regal prerogative, ſanctioned by the fundamental principles of the conſtitution, by all thoſe memorable precedents which form its firſt features, and by which the juſt and virtuous ſtruggles of our anceſtors, recognized by ſucceſſive generations, point out to their poſterity when they ought to interpoſe, and how long they ought to ſuffer. In his words, whoſe name reſts unknown, but whoſe fame is immortal, * we deſire "that the conſtitution may preſerve its monarchical form, but we would have the manners of the people purely and ſtrictly republican." Are you not ſenſible that this cry of republicaniſm, as the clamour againſt Catholic delegation, has been raiſed and prolonged by the miſchievous malignity of the lower goſſips of government, merely to drown the general voice for reform, like the ſtate manœuvre which ordered a flouriſh of trumpets, and alarum of drums, at the ſide of ſuffering patriots, when they wiſhed to addreſs themſelves to the reaſon and juſtice of the people.—But we will ſpeak and you will hear.—Yes, countrymen, we do deſire that extended liberty which may allow you, as citizens, to do what you will, provided you

* Junius.

do nor injure another, or rather to do all the good you can to others, without doing injuſtice to yourſelves. Yes, countrymen, we do wiſh for an equality of rights which is conſtitutional, not an equality of property which is impoſſible. Yes, countrymen, we do long for another equality, and we hope yet to ſee it realized: an equality conſiſting in the power of every father of a family to acquire by labour either of mind or body, ſomething beyond a mere ſubſiſtance, ſome little capital to prove, in caſe of ſickneſs, old age, or misfortune, a ſafeguard for his body and for his ſoul, a hallowed hoard that may lift him above the hard neceſſity which ſtruggles between conſcience and corruption; that may keep his heart whole and his ſpirit erect, while his body bends beneath its burden; make him fling away the wages of venality, and proudly return to an humble home, where a conſtitution that looks alike on the palace and the hovel, may ſtand at his hearth a tutelar divinity, and ſpread the Egis of equal law to guard him from the revenge of thoſe who offered the bribe and offered it in vain. Yes, Iriſhmen, we do proclaim it our deareſt wiſh, to ſee a more equal diſtribution of the benefits and bleſſings of life through the loweſt claſſes of the community, the ſtamina of ſociety; and we aſſert it as our firm belief, that an equal diſtribution of the elective franchiſe muſt contribute to this end; for national happineſs depends upon employment, which muſt itſelf ſpring from induſtry; and that again depends on liberty, ſecurity of perſon and property, equal law, ſpeedy and impartial juſtice, and, in ſhort, on that tenure in the ſtate, which may raiſe the community in relative value as in ſelf-eſtimation; make the agency of the People inſtrumental to a good government, and the re-agency of good Government meliorate the morals and manners of the People; bind together the distinct, and hitherto contending classes of society, by the cement of reciprocity and the interchange of obligations, and make the higher ranks—ballustrades that adorn the arch—feel their dependence on the people, who are the piles that support it. On the whole, we are so far republicans, as to desire a national House of Commons, in its origin, its form, its features, and its spirit; reverencing the people, not conspiring, with every other rank, against them, against their privileges, their pleasures, their homely happiness, their fireside enjoyment; but rather cherishing the elective franchise, the poor man's ewe lamb, and stigmatizing the landlord, who would despoil him of it, as a traitor to the constitution, a robber of national right, and a murderer of public happiness.

We have addressed the Friends of the People in England, and have received their concurrence, their thanks, and their gratulation.—We have addressed the Volunteers.—Deliverers of this injured land!—Have we done wrong?—if we have, tear your colours from the staff,—reverse your arms,—muffle your drums,—beat a funeral march for Ireland,—and then abandon the Corpse to Fencibles, to Militia, to Invalids, and dismounted Dragoons. If we have not done wrong,—and we swear by the Revolution of 82 that we have not,—go on with the zeal of enterprizing virtue, and a sense of your own importance, to exercise that Right of self-defence, which belongs to the Nation,—and to infuse constitutional energy into the public will, for the public good.

We now address Ireland.—We address you as a moral person, having a conscience, a will, and an understanding,—bound not only to preserve, but to perfect your nature,—the nations around you to witness your conduct, and a God above you to reward your virtues, or to punish your crimes. We speak to you as Man to Man,—reading your countenance—remarking the various passions that now shift across it, and striving to recollect a character long obliterated by foreign influence, or, after short and fierce developements, becoming the same dull blank as before. Severed as you have always been into counteracting interests,—an English interest, an Aristocratic interest, a Protestant interest, and a Catholic interest,—all contradistinguished from common-weal; and all, like the four elements, before Wisdom moved on the surface of the deep, exerting their respective influences to retain a chaos rather than create a Constitution: Actuated, as you have most generally been, by circumstances merely *external*,—compressed at one time into fortuitous union by the iron circle of British domination.—at another time, by the panic of invasion and fear of famine, when a bankrupt merchantry and embarrassed gentry, were starved into the common cause of a beggared People, whom Government had first pillaged, and then abandoned;—at the present time, perhaps impelled chiefly by the extraordinary events that have taken place on the Continent, it is not surprising that your real character is still, in a great measure, unknown to Europe, to Britain, and even to yourself. It is not surprising, that recollecting the past, we should be anxious about the future;—that we will not entirely confide in the fugitive splendor of the moment, the passing spirit of the people, or even the miraculous conversion of Parliament;—never,—never satisfied or secure, until we see a real Representation of that People in that Parliament;—until we can ſee Britain and Ireland connected by conſtitution, not by corruption,—by equal, not by ſtrong government;—until we ſee Public opinion, or the Will of the Nation, not as now, acting with rude and intermittent ſhocks, but the ſettled and central ballance of the political order, around which, without apparent motion in itſelf, the different branches of the Legiſlature may revolve with the ſilence and regularity of the planetery ſyſtem.

We addreſs your underſtanding,—the common ſenſe of the common-weal, and we aſk you, is it not a TRUTH, that where the People do not participate in the Legiſlature, by a delegation of repreſentatives, freely, fairly, and frequently elected, there can be no public liberty? Is it not the FACT, that in this country there is no repreſentative Legiſlature; becauſe the People are not repreſented in the Legiſlature, and have no partnerſhip in the Conſtitution? If it be the principle of the Conſtitution, that it is the right of every commoner in this realm to have a vote in the election of his Repreſentative; and that without ſuch vote, no man can be actually repreſented, it is our wiſh, in that caſe, to renovate that conſtitution, and to revive its ſuſpended animation, by giving free motion and full play to its vital principle. If, on the other hand, the conſtitution does *not* fully provide for an impartial and adequate repreſentation of all the People; if it be more excluſive than incluſive in its nature; if it be a monopoly, a privilege, or a prerogative; in that caſe is our deſire to *alter* it; for what is the Conſtitution to us, if we are as nothing to the Conſtitution? Is the Conſtitution made for you, or you for it? If the People do not conſtitute a part of it, what is it to them more than the ghoſt of Alfred; and what are principles without practice which they hear and read, to practice without principles which they see and feel?

The people of Ireland want political power:—taxation without consent, and legislation without representation, is not a partial grievance, or a Catholic grievance, but the grievance of the nation. The elective franchise is with-held from all, while all want a constituency in the constitution. The disfranchised, and the unfranchised, the unrepresented, and the misrepresented, the Catholic and the Presbyterian, are equally under the law, and out of the constitution: the Protestant, who is supposed to have it, and the Catholic who wishes to have it, are equally interested in having it free; for the truth is, that the whole community wants that emancipation which is necessary to a Free Government; we can give no truer definition of slavery, than that state in which men are governed without their consent, and no better description of freedom, than that not only those who make the law, should be bound by the law, but those who are bound by the law should have a share in the making it.

All Ireland knows and feels that the people are cursed from their own constitution, and that in a Government where they have no participation, the King must become a despot, and the Nation a slave. Public reason is convinced, and we assert with the confidence of conviction, that there are not 100 in this island, inimical to a renovation of the genuine constitution, who are not, at the same time, personally interested in the continuance of its corruptions and the prolongation of its abuses. The time is come when the Nation must speak for the Nation, and the long expected hour of redemption approaches, perhaps providentially protracted, until the universal voice could be heard, and the universal WILL declared. The Nation is ONE: one in body, one in soul, an union of colours in a single ray of truth; and the same inextinguishable principle which has accomplished many bloodless revolutions in our history; the peaceful revolution of 79, which gained a Free Trade, the peaceful revolution of 82, which gained an independence of right to Ireland; will consummate her imperfect freedom, with equal safety, honor and tranquillity, by the same means, a constitutional interposition of the people, justifiable by law, reason, right and expediency. The honor of Ireland, her dearest interests, present and future, the interest of her land-holders, and of her merchants, her commercial credit, her staple manufacture, are all involved in the present crisis, and urgently call upon you to declare in Convention, your wish, your will, and your determination; that the House of Commons may be restored to that true representative character which would regain national confidence, most effectually suppress all particular associations, give vigour to Government, and rest to the perturbed spirit of the people.

O, Ireland! Ireland! country to which we have clung in all our misfortunes, personal, religious, political; for whose freedom and happiness we are here solemnly united; for whom, as a society we live; and for whom as men, if hard necessity commands it, we are ready to die; let us conjure you not to abuse the present precious moment, by a self-extinguishment, by a credulous committal of your judgment and senses to the direction of others, by an idle and ideot gaze on what may be going on in parliament. In receiving good offices from all, distinguish between sound

Hibernicifm and that windy patriotifm, which is now puffing and blowing in the race of popularity. Truft as little to your friends as to your enemies in a matter where you can act only by yourfelves. The will of the Nation muft be declared before any Reform ought to take place. It is not therefore any clafs however numerous, any fociety however refpectable, any fubaltern affembly that have either right or competency to exprefs that authoritative will. Nothing lefs than the people can fpeak for the people. This competency refides not in a few freeholders fhivering in the corner of a county hall, but only in the whole community reprefented *in* each county, (as at prefent in Antrim,) by parochial delegation, and then *from* each county by baronial delegation, to provincial conventions, the union of which muft form the aweful will of the people of Ireland. Let us therefore conclude, by conjuring the county meetings now affembling to follow the example of Ulfter, and by appointing delegates to a Convention of their refpective provinces, to unite their fcattered and infulated wills into one momentous mafs, which may have authority fufficient to make a declaration of rights in behalf of the Nation. Then will the Sovereign gracioufly interpofe on the petition of all the people; the reality as well as form of good Government will be eftablifhed; the juftice of the conftitution vindicated; and when all this complicated fyftem of national fervitude and perfonal oppreffion, of perverted principle, and bafe practice, fhall be done away, men fhall exceedingly wonder how a Nation that boafted of a free conftitution, and the benignity of its laws, could have fuffered itfelf to be loaded fo long with a burthen fo grievous and infupportable.

February 10, 1793.

UNITED IRISHMEN OF DUBLIN.

Hon. SIMON BUTLER, Chairman.

OLIVER BOND, Secretary.

At a Meeting ſpecially convened to receive the report of the Committee appointed to enquire into the tendency of the war with France,—of the raiſing of the Militia,—and of the bill now pending in Parliament, for preventing the importation of Arms and Gun-powder into this Kingdom, and the removing and keeping of Gun-powder without licence,

The following Report was received and adopted:

THAT whatever pretexts may be held out, the real objects of the war about to be declared againſt France, appear to this Society to be not merely to puniſh crimes, but to perſecute principles; not merely to protect the allies of theſe kingdoms, but to produce a counter-revolution in France; not merely to check the progreſs of republicaniſm in Great-Britain and Ireland, but to ſtop the progreſs of liberty throughout Europe; and this Society is convinced, that this war would never be carried on, if it did not tend to effectuate a treaty, or rather a conſpiracy, entered into by tyrants and abettors of tyranny, when France had committed no crime, unleſs the emancipation of 24 millions of men be one.

That it appears to this Society, that a war,

which muſt be chiefly waged at ſea, and which, however ſucceſsful, can ſcarcely be maintained except to the ruin of commerce, is peculiarly dangerous to this iſland, the proſperity of which depends almoſt entirely upon its trade, and the commercial credit and confidence of which, have already been inſidiouſly ſhaken to a degree which every merchant and trader feels, and which ſeveral of its infant manufactures have lamentably experienced.

That this Society firmly attached from ſerious deliberation and conviction to a reform in the repreſentation of the people in parliament, and to a government by king, lords and commons, cannot but come forward publicly to expreſs its diſapprobation and ſorrow at a war, the tendency of which, if ſucceſsful, muſt be to perpetuate inveterate abuſes, and if unfortunate, may lead to the eſtabliſhing of ſyſtems of government untried in this country, and the apprehenſion of which, is alledged as a principal reaſon for engaging in hoſtility.

That it appears to this Society, not only inexpedient, but an infatuation amounting almoſt to madneſs, to ſubject Ireland, labouring under grievances hardly ſubmitted to in time of peace, to the invaſion of men, who profeſs to carry along with them " not fire and ſword but liberty." And if a war with France be in truth unavoidable, a redreſs of thoſe grievances, more peculiarly by a *total* emancipation of the Catholics, and by a radical reform in parliament, ought to be conſidered as an indiſpenſible *preliminary*.

That it appears to this Society, that the tendency of raiſing the militia in this kingdom, is to inveſt an ever-graſping adminiſtration with an enormous and alarming patronage, to extend its influence wide beyond the walls of parliament, and to diffuſe corruption through all claſſes of the people.

That it has alſo another afflicting tendency, namely, to repreſs, and if poſſible, to deſtroy the Volunteer inſtitution, by which this iſland was once before defended in time of war, and to which we again look, almoſt excluſively, for the protection of ourſelves and of our conſtitution, in the awful criſis that awaits us.

That it appears to be intended by the bill now depending in parliament, entitled, " a bill to " prevent the importation of arms and gun-" powder into this kingdom, and the removing " and keeping of gun-powder without licence," to prohibit the importation into this country of arms, ammunition, gun-powder or military ſtores, by any of his Majeſty's ſubjects, under the penalty of forfeiture of the ſame, and alſo of the ſum of £500: a precaution which cannot but appear extremely ſingular at the commencement of a war; a period, when it is the uſual policy of ſtates to encourage the importation of all articles neceſſary or defence, and to diſcourage their exportation; and the only exception to this extraordinary prohibition, is a particular and ſpecial licence, difficult to be obtained, and which may be refuſed.

That it appears to this Society, that the palpable tendency of this bill is to enact, *as againſt the whole body of the people*, the rigour of that penal code, reſpecting the keeping and uſing of arms, which it is profeſſed, is intended to be partially repealed, as in favour of the Catholics.

That in order to carry this into effect, it is intended by this bill to enact, that no perſon ſhall remove from any part of this kingdom, to any other part of this kingdom, any arms, ammunition, gun-powder or military ſtores, without a ſpecial and particular licence, under the penalty of a forfeiture of the ſame, and of £500.

That this Society is not aware what interpretation will hereafter be put upon the words "from "any part of this kingdom to any other part "of this kingdom," as that may depend upon the charge of a corrupt judge, or the verdict of a packed jury; but in ſtrictneſs of conſtruction, no man will be warranted, under this bill, to remove his firelock from his city to his country reſidence, or even perhaps from one chamber to another, or to take it down from his chimney and fire it at a houſe-breaker, without a ſpecial licence.

That by this bill it is intended to inflict on each act (which it conſtitutes a crime without conſidering the intention of the agent) at leaſt the penalty of £500, paying no regard to the nature of the act, or the ſituation and circumſtances of the party, and which, in its execution, will to a large majority of the nation amount to *perpetual impriſonment*.

That by this bill it appears intended to empower every juſtice of peace, without information upon oath, at his diſcretion, whenever he may think proper, at any hour of the day or night, forceably to enter and to ſearch the houſe of any of his Majeſty's ſubjects.

That according to the proviſions of this bill, it may not be in his Majeſty's clemency to remit the penalty or forfeiture incurred under it, in as much as any common informer may ſue for the ſame.

That this Society cannot be much conſoled by reading that this bill is to expire at the end of the next ſeſſion of parliament after the 1ſt. of

January 1794, when it reflects, that many of the oppressive acts, which still continue to disgrace our statute-book, had their commencements as *temporary laws*, and were ever afterwards most shamefully suffered to receive their continuances in silence.

That although this bill is pretended to be grounded on the late tumultuous risings in some parts of this kingdom, and the clandestine importation and secret keeping of arms, ammunition, gun-powder and military stores, its concealed but direct object appears to this Society to be, like the militia bill, to put down the Volunteers of Ireland, by rendering their array utterly impracticable.

That this Society would recommend it to certain members of parliament, who call themselves Patriots, because they are in Opposition, to watch over the welfare of the nation, and if they have not endeavoured to prevent its being involved in a war which must be ruinous to its commerce, and may probably prove destructive either of its liberty or of its constitution; at least to protect it from a militia, calculated, while it strengthens the standing vice of our government, to overbear the saviours of their country, and to avert from it the grievous oppressions of a bill, which contravenes every principle of penal law, and which for atrocity is scarcely paralelled even by any of the statutes enacted against the Catholics of Ireland. And this Society would submit to those gentlemen, whether by so doing they will not better fulfil their duty to their constituents, and better save themselves from becoming subjects of dupery and derision to their enemies, and of melancholy pity to their friends, than by *calumniating* an institution, the objects of which are more upright and constitutional than even the principles they *profess* to maintain, and the members of which are not chargeable with any tergiversation of conduct.

Friday, March 1st, 1793.

HOUSE OF LORDS.

THE Hon. SIMON BUTLER and Mr. OLIVER BOND appeared at the Bar in pursuance of their summonses.

Lord *Mountjoy* proposed, that the following paper, which he had read on the night preceding, and which had the names of the persons at the bar prefixed to it, should be submitted to their inspection.

" *24th February, 1793.*

" UNITED IRISHMEN OF DUBLIN.

" *Hon. SIMON BUTLER, Chairman.*

" *OLIVER BOND, Secretary,*

" WHEN a Committe of Secrecy was first appointed by the House of Lords, to enquire into the causes of the risings in certain counties of this kingdom; although this Society well foresaw the danger of abuse, to which such an institution was subject, yet it was restrained from expressing that opinion by the utility of the *professed* object, and by the hope, that the presence and advice of the two first Judicial Officers of this country, would prevent that Committee from doing those illegal acts, which less informed men might in such a situation commit.

" But since it has thought fit to change itself, from a Committee to enquire into the risings in certain counties of this kingdom, into an Inquisition, to scrutinize the private principles and secret thoughts of individuals; since it has not confined itself to simple enquiries and voluntary informations, but has assumed the right, and exercised the power of compelling attendance, and enforcing answers upon oath to personal interrogatories, tending to criminate the party examined: since its researches are not confined to the professed purposes of its institution, but directed principally to the discovery of evidence in support of prosecutions *heretofore commenced*, and utterly unconnected with the cause of the tumults it was appointed to investigate; since in its proceedings it has violated well ascertained principles of law, this Society feels itself compelled to warn the public mind, and point the public attention to the following observations:

" That the House of Lords can act only in a Legislative or Judicial capacity.

" That in it's Legislative capacity it has no authority to administer an oath.

" That in it's Judicial capacity it has a right to administer an oath; but that capacity extends only to error and appeal, except in cases of impeachment and trial of a peer, in which alone the House of Lords exercises an original jurisdiction.

" That the House of Lords, as a *Court*, has no right to act by *delegation*.

That the Committee of Secrecy possesses no authority, but what it derives by *delegation* from the House of Lords.

" That as the Houſe of Lords does not poſ-ſeſs *juriſdiction* in the ſubject matter referred to the Committee; and as, even if it did, it could not *delegate* the ſame, it neceſſarily follows, that the Committee has not judicial authority, and cannot adminiſter an oath.

" That even if the Committee of *Secrecy* acted as a *Court*, it's proceedings ought not to be ſecret.

" That no court has a right to exhibit perſonal interrogatories upon oath, the anſwers to which may criminate the party examined, except at the deſire of the party, and with a view to purge him from a contempt.

" That it was the principal vice of the Courts of High Commiſſion and Star Chamber, to examine upon perſonal interrogatories to convict the party examined; and that thoſe courts were aboliſhed, becauſe their proceedings were *illegal*, *unconſtitutional* and *oppreſſive*."

This paper was accordingly delivered into the hands of Mr. Butler, by the Gentleman Uſher —after he had ſeen it, he was aſked by Lord *Mountjoy*, if that paper, bearing his name, was printed by his directions or authority?

Mr. Butler ſaid, that the paper contained a Declaration of the Society of United Iriſhmen of the City of Dublin, and bore date the 24th February, 1793,——that he preſided at the Meeting——that as Chairman he put the queſtion on the ſeveral paragraphs, according as they were handed to him by the Committee which had been appointed to prepare them,——that he was then, and is ſtill ſatisfied, that every paragraph of that declaration was agreeable to law, and the principles of the conſtitution.

Lord *Mountjoy* ſaid, that Mr. Butler had not yet anſwered, whether he authorized the publication?

Mr. Butler replied, that he meant to give the fulleſt information on the ſubject, he did authorize the publication, he authorized it in common with every individual of the Society.

Mr. Bond was then interrogated——he was aſked whether he had ſigned the paper,—he replied that neither he nor Mr. Butler had ſigned the paper.—The reſolutions of this Society are referred to the Committee of Correſpondence for publication.—The Committee cauſe the names of the Chairman and Secretary to be prefixed to every publication.—That as Secretary he delivered this declaration to the Committee of Correſpondence.——And, on being aſked, by Lord *Clonmell*, whether he delivered it to the Committee for the purpoſe of publication, and whether he thereby authorized the publication, he replied in the affirmative.

Lord *Chancellor* then aſked Mr. Butler, whether he had any thing further to add.—Mr. Butler ſaid, that he attended to anſwer queſtions, that if his Lordſhip had any queſtions, to aſk, he (Mr. Butler) was ready to anſwer.

Mr. Butler and Mr. Bond were ordered to withdraw, but not to leave the Houſe.

They were ſhortly afterwards again ordered to the Bar, and the following reſolutions, agreed to by the Houſe in their abſence, having been read, viz.

" That the ſaid paper was a falſe, ſcandalous, and ſeditious libel; a high breach of the privileges of this Houſe, tending to diſturb the public peace, and queſtioning the authority of this High Court of Parliament."

" That Simon Butler and Oliver Bond having confeſſed that they had authorized the ſame to be printed, ſhould be taken into cuſtody."

They were committed to the cuſtody of the Gentleman Uſher—and ordered to withdraw in ſuch cuſtody.

In ſome time afterwards they were brought to the Bar in cuſtody of the Gentleman Uſher.

The Lord *Chancellor*, after reciting the foregoing reſolutions, ſpoke to the following purport: " Simon Butler and Oliver Bond, you were called to the Bar to anſwer for a libel on this High Court of Parliament,—you have confeſſed that ſuch libel, which for its preſumption, ignorance and miſchievous tendency is unprecedented, was printed by your authority——you, Simon Butler, cannot plead ignorance in extenuation—your noble birth, your education, the honourable profeſſion to which you belong, his Majeſty's gown which you wear, and to which you now ſtand a diſgrace, gave you the advantages of knowledge, and are ſtrong circumſtances of aggravation of your guilt.—It remains for me to pronounce the Judgment of the Houſe, which is, that you, Simon Butler and Oliver Bond, be impriſoned Six Months in the gaol of Newgate; that each of you pay a fine to the King of £500, and that you are not to be diſcharged from your confinement till ſuch fine be paid."

They were then taken from the Bar, and in a ſhort time after, conveyed in a Coach to Newgate, under the eſcort of 50 or 60 Soldiers and directions of *Alderman Warren*.

March 1ſt, 1793.

AT A FULL MEETING OF THE SOCIETY OF UNITED IRISHMEN.

BEAUCHAMP BAGENALL HARVEY,
in the Chair.

THOMAS RUSSELL, Secretary.

RESOLVED UNANIMOUSLY,

THAT a Deputation of five do wait, as early as poſſible, on the Hon. SIMON BUTLER, and Mr. OLIVER BOND, to expreſs the feelings of this Society as Men, as Citizens, and as United Iriſhmen on the events of this day, to teſtify our warmeſt ſenſe of gratitude for their dignified and magnanimous avowal of the Reſolutions of this Society before the Houſe of Lords, and to pledge to them our lives, our fortunes, and our ſacred honour, that we will never forſake our Officers, nor abandon the poſt of legal and conſtitutional Principle which we and our Officers have hitherto maintained, unſhaken, unſeduced and unterrified.

Newgate, March 2, 1793.

The Deputation having waited on Mr. BUTLER and Mr. BOND, they returned the following Anſwer to the Society.

GENTLEMEN,

WE received with pride your approbation of our conduct—Our cauſe is honourable and juſt. Whatever precedents may be adduced from *Engliſh* Journals in *times antecedent to the Revolution and the Bill of Rights*, our ſufferings, unexampled for ſeverity, are unprecedented in *this Kingdom*, unwarranted by Law and inconſiſtent with the principles of the Conſtitution. We will, however, bear them with fortitude; and entertain the ſanguine hopes that as we have been the firſt, ſo we may be the laſt Victims of Arbitrary power in this Nation.

SIMON BUTLER.
OLIVER BOND.

March 3, 1793.

THE SOCIETY OF UNITED IRISHMEN OF DUBLIN.

TO THE PEOPLE OF IRELAND.

BEAUCHAMP BAGENALL HARVEY,
Chairman.

THOMAS RUSSELL, Secretary.

WE have often addreſſed you in *your* cauſe; ſuffer us for once to addreſs you in *our own*. Two of the officers of our Society have been thrown into a common priſon, for the diſcharge of their duty:—a procedure ſo extraordinary, demands that we ſhould lay before you the whole of that conduct which has brought upon the Society ſo ſtrong an exertion of power.

The Society of United Iriſhmen was formed in November, 1791. Their principles, their motives, and their objects, were ſet forth in their Declaration and their Teſt. At that period the ſpirit of this nation was at the loweſt ebb; the great religious ſects were diſunited, the Proteſtants were diſheartened and ſunk by the memorable defeat of their Convention in 1783; the Catholics, without allies or ſupporters, accuſtomed to look to adminiſtration alone for relief, dared ſcarcely aſpire to hope for the loweſt degree of emancipation, and even that hope was repelled with contumely and diſdain;—adminiſtration was omnipotent, oppoſition was feeble, and the people were—nothing.

Such was the ſituation of Ireland, when in Belfaſt and in Dublin two ſocieties were formed, for the purpoſe of effectuating an union of the religious ſects, and a parliamentary reform. From the inſtant of their formation a new æra commenced: the public has been rouzed from their ſtupor, the ancient energy of the land is again called forth, and the people ſeem determined, in the ſpirit of 82, to demand and to obtain their long loſt rights.

The firſt meaſure of the United Iriſhmen was, a declaration in favour of a full and complete emancipation of the Catholics.—What was the conſequence? The moment that great and oppreſſed body ſaw itſelf ſupported by a ſingle ally, they ſpurned the vile ſubjection in which they had been ſo long held, and with the heavy yoke of the Penal Laws yet hanging on their necks, they ſummoned their repreſentatives from the four provinces of the kingdom, and with the determined voice of millions they called upon their ſovereign for a total abolition of that abominable and bloody code: a code, the extent and ſeverity of which was firſt made known by a report ſet forth by this Society, and compiled by the knowledge and induſtry of that man, who is now the victim of his diſintereſted patriotiſm, and who in publiſhing to the world the abominations of intollerance, bigotry, and perſecution, has committed a ſin againſt corruption which can never be forgiven.

If the knowledge of that penal code has been uſeful, if the complete union of the religious ſects has been beneficial, if the emancipation of Catholics be good for Ireland, then may this Society claim ſome merit, and ſome ſupport, from their countrymen.

In 1791, there was not a body of Men in Ireland that ventured to ſpeak, or ſcarce to think, of reform. The utmoſt length that patriots of that day went, was to attack a few of the outworks of corruption—the Societies of United Iriſhmen ſtormed her in the citadel. They did not fritter down the public ſpirit, or diſtract the public attention, by a variety of petty meaſures; they were not afraid to clip the wings of peculation too cloſe, or to cut up the trade of parliament by the roots:—They demanded a parliamentary reform; and what has been the conſequence? The cry has been re-echoed from county to county, and from province to province, till every honeſt man in the nation has become ardent in the purſuit; and even the tardy and lingering juſtice of parliament has been forced into a recognition of the principle. If then reform be good for Ireland, this Society, which firſt renewed the purſuit of that great object, may claim ſome merit, and ſome ſupport from their countrymen.

At the opening of this ſeſſion every man thought that the unanimous wiſh of the nation on the two great queſtions muſt be gratified:—that the Catholics muſt be completely emancipated, and a radical reform in parliament effectuated; but this deluſion was ſoon removed. It was ſuddenly diſcovered, that it was neceſſary to have a *ſtrong Government* in Ireland; a war was declared againſt France, ruinous to the riſing proſperity of this country; 20,000 regular troops, and 16,000 militia, were voted, and the famous Gun-powder Bill paſſed, by the unanimous conſent of *all parties* in parliament; the Society of United Iriſhmen, a vigilant centinel for the public good, warned their countrymen of the danger impending over their liberty and their commerce; they knew in doing ſo they were expoſing themſelves to the fury of government, but they diſregarded their own private ſafety when the good of their country was at ſtake. They could not hope to ſtop theſe meaſures, for they had no power, but what they could they did, they lodged their ſolemn proteſt againſt them, before the great tribunal of the nation.

In the progreſs of the preſent ſeſſion, it was thought neceſſary by the Houſe of Lords to eſtabliſh a Secret Committee, to inveſtigate the cauſe of the diſturbances now exiſting in a few counties in this kingdom. The examination of ſeveral individuals having tranſpired, the Society of United Iriſhmen felt it their duty to ſtep forward again, and to give ſuch information to their countrymen as might be neceſſary for their guidance.—They ſtated a few plain principles, which they did then and do now conceive to be *ſound conſtitutional law*. But now the meaſure of their offences was full, and the heavy hand of power ſo long with-held, was to fall with treble weight upon their heads.—Their chairman, the Hon. Simon Butler, and their ſecretary, Mr. Oliver Bond, were ſummoned before the Houſe of Lords; they were called upon to avow or diſavow the publication; they avowed it at once with the ſpirit and magnanimity of men who deſerved to be free: for this they have been ſentenced, with a ſeverity unexampled in the parliamentary annals of this country, to be impriſoned in Newgate for Six Months, and to pay a fine of £500. each and to remain in priſon until the ſaid fines be paid. By this ſentence, two gentlemen, one of noble birth, of great talents, and elevated ſituation in an honourable profeſſion; the other, a merchant of the faireſt character, the higheſt reſpectability, and in great and extenſive buſineſs, are torn away from their families and connections, carried through the streets with a military guard, and plunged like felons into the common Gaol, where they are at this instant confined among the vilest malefactors, the dross and refuse of the earth, AND THIS SENTENCE WAS PRONOUNCED BY A BODY, WHO ARE AT ONCE JUDGES AND PARTIES, WHO MEASURE THE OFFENCE, PROPORTION THE PUNISHMENT, AND FROM WHOSE SENTENCE THERE LIES NO APPEAL.

We do not mention here criminal prosecutions instituted against several of our members in the courts of law for publishing and distributing our address to the Volunteers of Ireland; respect for the existing laws of our country, imposes upon us a silence which no provocation shall induce us to break, WE KNOW WHEN JURIES INTERVENE, THAT JUSTICE WILL BE DONE.

Such is the history of the Society, and such are the enormities which have drawn upon them the persecution upon which they now labour. Their prime offence is their devoted attachment to reform; an attachment, which in the eyes of a bad administration includes all political sin; their next offence, is an ardent wish for a complete and total, *not a partial and illusory, emancipation* of the Catholics. Their next offence is having published a strong censure on the impending ruinous war, on the militia and gun-powder acts; and finally, the crowning offence for which their officers now lie in gaol, by order of the House of Lords, is having instructed their countrymen in what they conceive to be the law of the land, for the guidance of those who might be summoned before the Secret Committee.

The Society now Submits to their countrymen a few plain facts:—The war has been approved by Parliament; 36,000 men have been voted—*to be employed in Ireland*; the Gun-powder Bill is passed; the Volunteers of Dublin have been insulted; their artillery has been seized; soldiers hourly are seen with a Police Magistrate at their head parading the streets, entering and searching the houses of Citizens for arms; and finally, the officers of the *only* Society which had spirit to observe on those proceedings, are seized and thrown into prison. This is what *has* been done, we will add what has *not* been done; a complete emancipation of the Catholics has *not* been granted, and a reform in Parliament has *not* been accomplished.

We have now submitted to our country the whole of our present situation; with that country it rests to decide upon our conduct; if they approve it, to testify their approbation; if they condemn it, to express that condemnation. The mode of doing the one or the other is obvious. In one province the people have already organized themselves, and declared their political creed. Let the other provinces follow their example. Let the National Convention then assemble and pronounce the National will. That will must have its due weight.

We may be after all wrong; our ardency in pursuit of constitutional liberty may be such as our countrymen have not yet spirit to follow; in that case we must desist, but we shall desist, not from conviction, but from despair. If Irishmen do not wish to see Catholics completely free; if they desire the continuance of inveterate abuse and corruption; if they dread a reform in the representation of the people; if they wish to behold an institution, once the pride and boast of Ireland, insulted, degraded, and plundered of their arms; if they are content to see men who have the spirit to step forward and aſſert the rights and privileges of their country, dragged away like felons, and thrown into the common gaol,—then is this Society wrong in its purſuits and in its practice.—We have no right to agitate with notions of liberty, now perhaps obſolete, a land which is determined to remain ſunk in the lethargy of corruption; it is our principle, that if a nation wills a bad government, it ought to have that government.—We have no power, and we have no right, to force men to be free.

Whatever be the determination of our countrymen, we will do our duty; if our principles ſhall meet with the approbation and ſupport of the nation nothing ſhall compel us to quit that line of conduct which our conſcience and our honor point out, and which we have hitherto endeavoured to purſue:—in the worſt event, whatever may be our fate, and the public determination, we ſhall ſteadily ſupport the men who are now, in the honourable diſcharge of their duty, ſuffering in the cauſe of this Society, of Liberty, and of Ireland.

June 7, 1793.

UNITED IRISHMEN OF DUBLIN.

HENRY SHEARES, President.

EDW. JOS. LEWINES, Secretary.

On Motion, the following Resolution of the CATHOLIC COMMITTEE was read:

"*RESOLVED that it is with pleasure and gra-*
"*titude, we have observed the House of Com-*
"*mons, in this Session, unanimously taking in-*
"*to their consideration, that most important*
"*measure, the present representation of the*
"*People in Parliament: and we do most ear-*
"*nestly exhort the Catholics of Ireland, to co-*
"*operate with their Protestant Brethren, in all*
"*legal and constitutional means to carry into*
"*effect, that great measure, recognized by the*
"*wisdom of Parliament, and so essential to the*
"*freedom, happiness and prosperity of Ireland*
"*—a Reform in the Representation of the*
"*People in the Commons House.*"

RESOLVED, that this Society do agree to the following ADDRESS to their CATHOLIC COUNTRYMEN.

FELLOW CITIZENS,

WE hasten to recognize, under this new and endearing title, a People tried by experience, and schooled by adversary, who have signalized their loyalty amidst all the rigours of the Law—who have proved their fidelity to a constitution which with respect to them violated all its own principles, and who have set an example of patient perdurance in religious faith, while for a century they experienced a persecution equally abhorrent from every maxim of good government, and every principle of genuine christianity. We congratulate our country on such a large addition to the public domain of mind, the cultivation and produce of which may in some degree compensate for past waste and negligence. We congratulate the Empire that the loss of three millions across the Atlantic is supplied by the timely acquisition of the same number at home. We congratulate the Constitution that new Life is transfused into its veins at a period of decay and decrepitude; and we trust that the Heroism which suffered with such constancy for the sake of religion, will now change into a Heroism that shall act with equal steadiness and consistency for the freedom, the honour and the independence of this country.

By the wise benevolence of the Sovereign, by the enlightened spirit of the times, by the union of religious persuasions for the good of civil society, by the spirit, prudence, and consistency of the Catholic Committee, who, during their whole existence, were true to the trust reposed in them, and whose last breath sanctified the expedience and necessity of a Parliamentary Reform; by these causes, along with other fortunate coincidences, you have been admitted into the outer court of the constitution. Look around you—but without superstitious awe, or idolatrous prostration, for the edifice you enter is not a Temple but a Dwelling. Enter therefore with erect heads, and yet with grateful hearts, grateful to your King, grateful to your Country, attached to the constitution by manly principle not by childish prejudice, faithful to your friends through every change either of their fortune or your own, and if not forgetful of the virulence of your enemies, having always the magnanimity to pity and to deſpiſe them.

Loving the conſtitution rationally, not adopted merely to its infirmities, loving it too well, to dote upon its abuſes, you muſt ſhortly be ſenſible, that, without reform, the balance of the elective franchiſe will be more off the centre than before, the inequality of popular repreſentation more glaring and monſtrous, the diſproportion more enormous between the number of electors in 32 counties, and that in the boroughs from which you are excluded. What was kept cloſe and corrupt before, will be cloſe and corrupt ſtill; common right will ſtill be private property: and the conſtitution will be impriſoned under the lock and key of corporations. The æra of your enfranchiſement will therefore eventually work the weal or woe of Ireland. We do truſt that you will not be incorporated merely with the body of the conſtitution without adding to its ſpirit. You are called into Citizenſhip not to ſanction abuſe, but to diſcountenance it, not to accumulate corruption but to meliorate manners and infuſe into ſociety purer practice and ſounder morality; always ſeparating in thought and action, *mis*-government and *mal*-adminiſtration from the good ſenſe and right reaſon natural to, and co-eval with the conſtitution; and always remembering that nothing can be good for any part of the nation which has not for its object the intereſt of the whole.

Fellow-Citizens.—We ſpeak to you with much earneſtneſs of affection, repeating with ſincereſt pleaſure, that tender and domeſtic appellation which binds us into one People. But what is it which has lately made and muſt keep us ONE? Not the ſoil we inhabit, not the language we uſe, but our ſingleneſs of ſentiment reſpecting one great political truth, our indivisible union on the main object of general interest—a Parliamentary Reform. This is the civic Faith for which this Society exists, and for which it suffers under a persecution that still, as of old, savage in its nature, though somewhat smoother in its form, wreaks its mighty vengeance on person and property, or exerts its puny malice to ruin us in the professions by which we live, merely for an undaunted adherence to a single good and glorious principle which has always animated our publications and will always regulate our practice. We conjure you, in the most solemn manner, to remember with the respect due to such authority, the last Words, the political Will and Testament of a body of men who have deserved so well of their constituents and of their Country. Never forget them. Never forsake them—Let this principle of Reform live in your practice, and give energy to the new character you are about to sustain for the glory or the disgrace of Ireland.

As for us, our particular sufferings as a Society are lost, at present, in an overwhelming sense of national calamity. We wish in our social, and individual capacities, to expedite every measure that has the remotest chance of giving the smallest relief to such urgent distress, lamenting at the same time that every means adopted must prove partial, palliative and inadequate, until the origin of the extended evil, be boldly looked to, and what is universally understood, is as plainly and publicly expressed. What then is the Cause? War. What is the Cure? Peace. What will prevent a relapse and perpetuate that health and soundness which it had restored? a *National* House of Commons, that would conform to the will of the people by the imposition of such duties as might secure, to Irish manufactures, a natural but not exclusive preference in an Irish market: a *National* House of Commons acting *from* and therefore *for* the People, not personating but representing them, not holding forth the Constitution merely as an object to provoke doubts, or excite terrors, speaking always in clouds, or by thunder; but writing the Law in the tablet of our hearts, rivetting the constitution into the common sense of the community, the basis from which it has shifted, and extinguished all discontent and disaffection by diffusing rational loyalty and the allegiance of convinced understanding.

We will never cease to dwell on this theme, for we wish to make the times conform to us, rather than to make our principles conform to the times. For the present, we lye just in the track of the pestilential wind of calumny which purposely confounds the reformer, the republican and the regicide; which preserves and propagates a panic of innovation and a distrust between man and man, in order to keep back internal union, at the dreadful sacrifice of commercial credit, of public revenue, and of national character. Even, at this moment, perhaps, a provident jealousy may be contriving means for our dispersion, naturally fearful that wherever two or three honest men are assembled together, their conversation must, at this time, turn on the oppressions of the subject, and the misery of this Country.

June 21ſt, 1793.

THE SOCIETY OF UNITED IRISHMEN

DUBLIN.

TO THE PEOPLE OF IRELAND.

HENRY SHEARES, Preſident.

WILLIAM LEVINGSTON WEBB, Sec.

WHEN the preſent War firſt threatened this Nation with the calamities, under which it has ſince groaned, and by which it is at this moment almoſt over-whelmed, we warned you of the approaching danger, and ſought by a timely caution to avert the conſequent ruin.—We told you it was a meaſure, fraught with deſtruction to your infant Manufactures, to your growing Commerce, and to your almoſt mature Spirit—How far the Prediction we then uttered has been juſtified by the event, let the ſurrounding miſeries of this Country determine—An expiring and nearly extinguiſhed Credit—the Pride of Commerce humbled and diſgraced—the cries of Famine re-echoed thro' encreaſing thouſands of your Manufacturers, diſcarded from the exerciſe of their honeſt labour, driven into penury and inaction; and compelled to ſeek an uncertain ſubſiſtence from the humanity of their more affluent, tho' leſs induſtrious Fellow-citizens. Such are the effects, and ſuch were the predicted conſequences of a War, commenced without provocation, and which, if ſuffered to continue a few Months longer, muſt inevitably produce national Shame, national Bankruptcy, and national Destruction.

We declared that the persecution of Principles, was the real object of the War, whatever pretexts may be held out. Judge of this assertion also by the event—Behold the external invasion against Liberty seconded by internal outrages on your most valued Rights—Behold your band of Patriots, once embodied and exulting in the glorious cause of Freedom; once the Pride of IRELAND, and the admiration of attentive Europe, your Volunteers now insulted and disarmed—Behold your loved, your revered, your idolized Palladium, the tryal by Jury, profaned and violated: trampled in the dust by the unhallowed foot of undefined Privilege—Behold your faithful Friends, for daring to step forward in your defence, dragged to a loathsome Prison, and loaded with every injury, which falsehood and tyranny could suggest.

Imposed upon through the medium of a generous sensibility, falsely and designedly excited to entrap you, you too slightly regarded the salutary caution of your Friends; and though your reason and your interests revolted at the War, you suffered in silence that pernicious measure to be adopted—Again we stepped forward; for we have no pride, but in the conscious discharge of duty. We attempted to alleviate the miseries we could not avert. Foreseeing the dreadful state of abandonment, into which an interruption of Commerce must throw the most useful and industrious part of the community, we held forth an example to the public, which, if then followed, would have lessened and postponed that inevitable calamity—We publicly and solemnly pledged ourselves to the exclusive consumption of Irish Manufactures, and called on our fellow-citizens, by uniting in a ſimilar reſolution to afford the only relief then in their power to beſtow. Yet even this act of Patriotiſm and Humanity ſupplied calumny with encreaſe of poiſon; in endeavouring to forewarn our Countrymen of all the dangers and miſeries, which at this inſtant ſhake private happineſs and public ſafety to their centres, we were repreſented as acting from malignant motives, and as ſeeking, by alarming the public mind with groundleſs apprehenſions, to agitate it to outrage—With ſilent contempt we liſtened to the baſe ſuggeſtion, for it was not worthy our reſentment. We knew that thoſe, who had doomed this unhappy Country to its preſent ſufferings, would at laſt be compelled to adopt the palliatives ſince they had rejected the preventives we at firſt propoſed: We knew that they would be forced to ſtop the cries of clamorous famine, by taking up the precedent we had ſet them, and to fly to theſe means of appeaſing the deſperate reſentment of ſtarving thouſands, which they had before reprobated as the inſtrument of exciting it.

What has been the caſe? Although the War has yet exiſted but a few months, it's dire effects have already pierced the very marrow of Society—Thoſe indeed, who adviſed to plunge you into all it's horrors, have not ſuffered the ſlighteſt inconveniencies: but is there an Artificer of any deſcription, a Manufacturer of any denomination, a ſingle Iriſhman who lives by his honeſt induſtry, who has not wholly or in part been deprived of his means of ſuſtenance? All export is deſtroyed, except the export of Specie, wrung from the hard hand of labour to pamper the luxury of Abſentees——Every trade is ſuſpended, except the trade of Corruption, which flouriſhes by the impoveriſhment of this devoted ſoil——

At length this city is ſummoned to deviſe the beſt means to alleviate the preſſing miſery, and guard againſt the growing danger. In it's deciſion is recorded the public approbation of thoſe meaſures our provident anxiety firſt ſuggeſted—It is from the verdict of our fellow-citizens alone that we have met or wiſh to meet redreſs againſt Calumny and Outrage—To their tribunal we alone appeal—at their tribunal we alone find juſtice.

What has hitherto been attempted for your relief, is but of a nature temporary and tranſient. Diſeaſe and pain will again recur, and with redoubled force, unleſs you trace the evil to it's ſource and rectify it there. Dare then, Citizens of Ireland, to look your ſituation in the face. Shrink not from the touch of truth, but with a manly fortitude effectuate your cure, however painful the neceſſary operation—Since even thoſe members of oppoſition, in whom you have hitherto fooliſhly and fatally confided, have abuſed that confidence, deſerted your intereſts, and ſupported this deſtructive meaſure; it is your right, and it is your duty to act for yourſelves in this great criſis. Aſſemble in your Pariſhes, in your Towns, in your Counties and in your Provinces, there ſpeak forth your ſentiments, and let your will be known—With the firm voice of injured millions require a Peace—Purſue the example of the Catholic Convention—Unite order with ſpirit, tranquillity with action——Like them, carry your wiſhes to the throne itſelf, and fear not for their ſucceſs—But like them, whilſt you ſeek a remedy for your preſent ſufferings, ever remember that a radical Reform in the ſyſtem of repreſentation is the only means of avoiding a repetition of them—Call on your King to chain down the monſter War, which has devoured your Commerce: which gorges it's hateful appetite by preying on the wretchedneſs of your Manufactures, and enſlaving them for life, the inſtruments of tyranny and ſlaughter—Call on him to ſpurn from his counſels thoſe, who ſhall aſſert that you are bound to rob and to be robbed, to murder and to be murdered, to inflict and to endure all the complicated miſeries of War, becauſe an unfeeling policy ſhould dictate the horrid act—Call on him to give you Peace—But would you render permanent it's bleſſings, when obtained?—Would you add vigour to your Agriculture, to your Manufactures, and to your Commerce?—Would you ſecure to yourſelves the produce of your various labours, now conſumed by oppreſſive and encreaſing taxes; by placemen without employment, and penſioners without merit? Reform your preſent ſtate of repreſentation by an infuſion of purity and health into your Commons Houſe—Hold forth to your Sovereign the records of Parliament, and let him read therein the incompetence of it's exiſting form—He has already partially acknowledged the fact, and failed not to eſpouſe the People's Cauſe.——He will ſee, and with the ſame ingeniouſneſs he will avow, that thoſe repeated neceſſities for your perſonal interference prove the evil of which you complain—From his candour and from his juſtice, you have every thing to hope, you have nothing to fear.

AT A SPECIAL MEETING OF THE SOCIETY OF UNITED IRISHMEN,

Held on the 15th of JULY,

For the Purpose of taking into Consideration the BILL *now depending in* PARLIAMENT, *entitled, " A Bill to prevent the Election or " other Appointment of Conventions or other " unlawful Assemblies, under pretence of pre- " paring or presenting Public Petitions, or " other Addresses to his Majesty or the Par- " liament."*

The following Resolutions were unanimously agreed to, *viz.*

HENRY SHEARES, President

WILLIAM LEVINGSTON WEBB, Sec.[y]

RESOLVED,

THAT it is, and ever has been the indubitable right of the People of this country to assemble and consult together, for the purpose of instructing their Representatives, or of petitioning any branch of the Legislature, concerning such measures, as may in any manner affect their interests.

THAT, since that part of our ancient Constitution, which made the office of Sheriff elective by the People, has been changed, it has too frequently occurred, that Sheriffs, although required according to law to summon meetings for those purposes, have either wholly refused to comply with such requisitions, or complied therewith in such a manner, as purposely to defeat the objects, for which those meetings were summoned: unless agreeable to the views of those, to whose influence they were indebted for their office.

THAT in the actual exercise of this right, many of those evils have also occurred, which necessarily attach upon numerous and popular meetings, to the prejudice of cool deliberation and public tranquillity.

THAT in order to avoid those evils, and yet preserve the deliberative right of the People in it's full force and efficacy, the appointment of Delegates from Parishes, Towns, or other portions of the People, chosen from amongst themselves for their virtue and talents, appears to us most consonant to reason and good policy, and most conducive to the preservation of peace and public order.

THAT we cannot attribute any other motives to the *Roman Catholics* of this Country, in pursuing the system above-mentioned, in order to collect the opinions of three millions of People on the subject of their dearest interests, than those of a laudable anxiety, for the maintenance of public tranquillity, and the highest reverence for the Laws and Constitution of their Country: As we are persuaded, that had their conduct evinced any thing inimical to those, it would not have received the sanction of royal approbation, or parliamentary indulgence.

THAT the scrupulous decorum, observed in the appointment and conduct of the *Catholic* Committee, and the success which crowned their labours with the restitution of Constitutional Rights, are in our eyes incontestible proofs, that the Syſtem by which that Committee was created, and that which it purſued were ſtrictly conformable to the Laws of the Land, and merit the praiſe and imitation of this entire Nation.

THAT we cannot avoid expreſſing our apprehenſions at the introduction of a Bill into Parliament, which appears to us, as tending to deprive the People of this Country of the moſt effectual mode of expreſſing and collecting their opinions, whenever they ſhall think it neceſſary to inſtruct their Repreſentatives, or petition any branch of the Legiſlature: and we moſt earneſtly warn and exhort our Fellow-citizens of *Ireland*, ſpeedily to aſſemble in their Cities and Counties, for the purpoſe of conſidering a ſubject, which involves their deareſt intereſts, and of communicating to their Repreſentatives the reſult of their deliberations, or petitioning their Sovereign to refuſe his royal aſſent to that alarming meaſure.

July 26, 1794.

UNITED IRISHMEN.

HENRY SHEARES *having been requested to leave the Chair,*

JAMES DIXON, Chairman.

WILLIAM LEVINGSTON WEBB, Sec.

The following Publication was read,

"TO THE PUBLIC.

THE following Paragraph appeared in the FREEMAN'S JOURNAL on *Saturday* 20th inst. and afterwards in other Prints, as a part of the Lord Chancellor's Speech in the House of Lords.

PARAGRAPH.

" *There were in* Dublin *two persons who were*
" *Members of the* French Jacobin Club,
" *and who, his Lordship believed were in*
" *the pay of that Society to foment sedition*
" *in this Country. One of their names ap-*
" *peared at the head of a printed paper*
" *published last month by the* UNITED IRISH-
" MEN, *to which Society they also belonged.*

On perusal of the above Paragraph, I wrote the following Letter to his Lordship.

MY LORD,

HAVING this day seen in the Public Prints of yesterday, a gross and infamous calumny, which, from the ſtrength of it's alluſions, I cannot avoid conſidering as directed againſt me, I think it incumbent on me to addreſs myſelf to your Lordſhip, prior to taking any ſtep towards the puniſhment of it's author.

I AM induced to take this liberty, my Lord, from the circumſtances of your Lordſhip's name having been made uſe of (falſely I am perſuaded) to ſanction the malignant falſhood contained in that publication.—It is therein aſſerted, that your Lordſhip, in the Houſe of Lords, repreſented me as a Member and Agent of the *Jacobin Club* in *France*, and employed by them to foment ſedition in this Country:—An aſſertion, which I am bound to believe as ill founded in relation to your Lordſhip, as I know it to be falſe in reſpect to me.—Aſſuring your Lordſhip of my perfect conviction, that ſuch an accuſation could never have proceeded from the alledged ſource, I take the liberty of requeſting that your Lordſhip will authorize me to aſſert, that the publication was unwarranted by any thing that fell from your Lordſhip, and that I may have your Lordſhip's permiſſion for ſuch legal proceeding againſt the publiſher as may ſeem adviſeable.

I am, my Lord, your Lordſhip's

moſt obedient,

Baggot-ſtreet, very humble Servant,

July 21, 1793. HENRY SHEARES.

Dublin, July 26, 1793.

HAVING received no anſwer to the above Letter, I deem it a duty I owe to myſelf, to the Society to which I belong, and to the Public in general, to lay the circumſtances of this tranſaction before the Nation.

HENRY SHEARES.

Reſolved, that HENRY SHEARES *be addreſſed by this* SOCIETY.

UNITED IRISHMEN TO HENRY SHEARES.

THIS Society is in it's choice of a Preſident, has been directed to you by it's conviction of your patriotic and Conſtitutional principles.

If by this mark of our reſpect and confidence, you have been expoſed to ſlander of the moſt ſingular and unwarrantable nature, you have derived this honorable diſtinction from the corrupt policy which has been uniformly employed to vilify the moſt virtuous aſſertors of their Country's Rights.

Convinced that the calumny, alluded to in your Letter to the Chancellor, is unfounded, and that the meanneſs which marks it, as well as it's malignity, renders it impoſſible for us to ſuppoſe, that it could have proceeded from the authority to which it had been imputed; but was rather the fabrication of a venal Print, which has long inſulted the moſt honorable and independent characters of the community, we earneſtly aſſure you, that we will co-operate with you in every mode of obtaining juſtice from the laws of your Country.

Amongſt us, nothing is ſecret, nothing under-hand——Our numbers, our independence, our individual characters might ſtand as teſts of our intentions.——We have every motive of attachment to the intereſt and happineſs of our Country.——The ſacrifice you make to public duty, can only ſerve to endear you to us more than ever.

To which HENRY SHEARES *gave the following Anſwer.*

UNITED IRISHMEN,

YOUR affectionate addreſs has made the deepeſt impreſſion on my heart.—I ſhall ever hope to deſerve it—That congenial principle which firſt led and attached me to you, has received, if poſſible, additional energy by this teſtimony of your approbation.—From the laws of my Country I have no doubt of redreſs—In contempt and defiance of calumny and oppreſſion, I will devote my life to the great cauſe for which we firſt united; confident, that by a firm adherence to the principles of our inſtitution, we ſhall proportionally effect the welfare and happineſs of our native Country.

August 12, 1793.

THE SOCIETY OF UNITED IRISHMEN OF DUBLIN.

To JAMES REYNOLDS, M. D.

HENRY JACKSON, Chairman.

MATT. DOWLING, Secretary.

WE thank you for your legal and constitutional resistance to an Examination on Oath before a Committee of the House of Lords. You rightly distinguished between the Power assumed by that Committee, and the legitimate Authority belonging to that House. The opinion of the soundest Lawyers in both Kingdoms sanctions this Distinction. In your Conduct mild but manly, in your Language gentle in the Letter but magnanimous in the Spirit, the obstinacy of Virtue and the pride of good Sense were well contrasted with fierce Precipitation, vulgar Manners, and ignoble Expression.

The Consequence was your Imprisonment for near five Months,—but this is not a Consequence that can ever destroy either political or moral Truth; and to a Mind like yours, filled with honest Energy, Confinement is but a Compression which serves to give it greater Elasticity. Committed at first for refusing to take an Oath, and enlarged at last though persisting in that Refusal, you have at once exposed the abuse of Power, its Error, and its Inconsistency. We thank you, Sir, for what you have done and suffered in the

Cauſe of your Country; and although this Country ſits at preſent a ſilent Spectator in torpid Aſtoniſhment at the bold Meaſures hazarded by bad frontleſs Men, and, at a Time when we are ſcarcely ſuffered to think as we pleaſe, much leſs to ſpeak as we think, even at ſuch a Time the *Society of United Iriſhmen* would deem it the ſame criminal Neutrality to conceal their cenſure where it was juſtly due, and to withhold from you, Sir, an equally juſt Approbation.

UNITED IRISHMEN.

ACCEPT the grateful acknowledgments of a Man whoſe warmeſt Wiſh is the Liberty and Happineſs of all his Species.

My Sentiments have ever been congenial with yours.—As an Iriſhman, I will ever be ready to reſiſt Oppreſſion, and actively purſue every Meaſure which may tend to the complete Emancipation of my Country.

JAMES REYNOLDS.

Friday, 16th August. 1793.

THE SOCIETY OF UNITED IRISHMEN OF

D U B L I N.

JOHN SHEARES, Chairman,

W. L. WEBB, Secretary,

TO THE HON. SIMON BUTLER

AND OLIVER BOND, Esq.

GENTLEMEN,

OUR DEAR AND RESPECTED FRIENDS!

ON the first of March we saw you enter into prison, with an air and manner that testified not only a serene and settled conviction in the justice of your cause, but a chearful confidence in your own fortitude to sustain all the consequences that an attachment to this cause might bring upon you;— and we now see you, after an imprisonment of six months, come out with the same unbending spirit; in the same health of body; with the same alacrity of mind; both preserved sound and unaltered, probably from the same cause, that vital energy which a sense of unmerited suffering, and the consciousness of doing our duty, never fail to communicate. It is this conscious sense of unmerited injury, that refreshes the soul amidst the closest confinement, blows up the spark of life, and invigorates both the head and the heart. This— which made Mirabeau write for Liberty in a dungeon, while his enemies conspired, against it in the anti-chamber; this—which expanded the soul of

Rawleigh, gave it power to wander at large, and, in ſpite of bars, in defiance of gaolers, to leave the narrow cell where his body lay, and write for poſterity—a Hiſtory of the World.

Notwithſtanding the irreſiſtible argument of ſix months impriſonment in a common gaol, we are ſtill inclined to lament, that the law and cuſtom of parliament ſhould have ever entered into a conteſt with the liberty of the preſs and the rights of the people; and that a diſcretionary power of puniſhment ſhould ſo often ſuperſede the ordinary courſe of criminal juriſdiction and the ſacred trial by jury. We continue ſtill inclined to believe, that all undefined and irreſponſible power, by whatever perſon or body aſſumed, is in it's nature deſpotic. The Vigilance of the people, and the cenſorſhip of the preſs, are the only means of guarding againſt it's deadening influence, and preſerving thoſe barriers which the ſpirit of free government ought to place between the legiſlative, executive, and judiciary departments. We ſtill think, that particular and anxious care ought to be taken, never to mingle and confound the legiſlative and judicial powers, for the conjunction is politically inceſtuous, and the production is always a monſter.

Gentlemen—your country is much your debtor. But we muſt ſuppoſe you by this time too well experienced in the mutability of public opinion, to expect that ſhe will, for the preſent, acknowledge the debt, much leſs—return the obligation; that ſhe will either ſympathiſe with what you have ſuffered, or partake in our heartfelt joy at your enlargement. Indeed you will ſcarcely now know your country, in a few months ſo much altered. Indiſpoſed to condole or to congratulate, deſponding without reaſon, exhauſted without effort, ſhe ſits on the ground, in a fit of mental alienation;

unconſcious of her real malady, ſcared at every whiſper; her thouſand ears open for falſehoods from abroad, her thouſand eyes ſhut againſt the truth at home; worked up by falſe ſuggeſtions and artful inſinuations, to ſuch a madneſs of ſuſpicion, as makes her miſtake her deareſt friends for her deadlieſt foes, and revile the only Society which ever purſued her welfare with ſpirit and perſeverance, as attempting at her life with the torch of an incendiary and the dagger of an aſſaſſin.

From a public, thus inquiſitive about the affairs of other people, thus incurious about its own, thus deluded, we were going to ſay, in language of high authority, thus *beſotted*, we appeal for your fame, and our own juſtification, to the ſame public, in a more recollected, a more ſober, a more dignified moment: when the periſhable politics of party in place, and party out of place, ſhall have paſſed away like the almanack of the year; when the light ſhall break in on an under-working *Family Compact*, whoſe buſineſs it has been to conceal the real ſituation and ſentiments of this country, from the immediate councils of the Sovereign; when a compromiſing, parlying, panic-ſtruck oppoſition, negotiating without authority, ſurrendering without condition, ſhall repent of their puſillanimous credulity; and, when the nation ſhall dare to acknowledge as a truth, what in it's conſcience it feels as a fact, that thoſe only are her friends who ſtand up while all are proſtrate around them, and call aloud on miniſtry and on oppoſition for Reform, radical, comprehenſive, immediate; ſuch as will nationalize liberty, and make this country ceaſe to be what it has been well deſcribed—" a heavy handed unfeelling ariſtocracy over a people ferocious and rendered deſperate by poverty and wretchedneſs." But if ſuch a time ſhould not ſoon arrive; if this country ſhould remain ſtill abuſed and contented ; there is a World elſewhere. Wherever Freedom is—*there* is our Country, and *there* ought to be our Home. Let this government take care. Let them think of depopulation, and tremble. Who makes the Rich ?—the Poor. What makes the ſhuttle fly, and the plough cleave the furrows ?—the Poor. Should the Poor emigrate, what would become of you, proud, powerful, ſilly men ?—What would become of you, if the ears of corn ſhould wither on the ſtalk, and the labours of the loom ſhould ceaſe ?—Who would feed you then if hungry, or clothe you when naked ? —Give the Poor a Country, or you will loſe one yourſelves. Mankind, like other commodities, will follow the demand ; and, if depreciated here below all value, will fly to a better market.

Gentlemen, we again ſalute you with great reſpect and affection, as Friends and Brothers. We ſalute you, in the unity of an honeſt and honourable cauſe. May you receive the reward of your ſufferings, and triumph in the Freedom of your Country.

August 16, 1793.

THE HON. SIMON BUTLER AND OLIVER BOND, Esq.

RETURNED THE FOLLOWING ANSWER:

WE received the honour of your ſpirited and affectionate Addreſs, with equal pride and gratitude. You have done juſtice to the feelings which have ſupported us under our impriſonment; and, if our ſituation required adventitious conſolation, the *patriotic* attention of our numerous friends has moſt amply ſupplied it. Our ſufferings have not warped our underſtandings: and we ſtill think, that we only diſcharge an indiſpenſible duty, while we treat all public topics with free diſcuſſion—preſerving a due reſpect for the public peace, and the laws of the land. We will only boaſt of our Conſtitution when it knows no power which is not reſponſible. Prerogative, founded upon the ſalutary maxim, that the King can do no wrong, held forth at all times ſome relief in the reſponſibility of the Miniſter; but Privilege, which arrogates to itſelf a like conſtitutional principle, precludes all reſource whatſoever againſt its illegal or arbitrary exerciſe, acknowledging no controul, no corrective, it regards not the forms of law; and while it remains undefined and irreſponſible, there is no ſafety in the land. We have thought it our duty to ſeek redreſs, but we ſought it in vain. We have not even received *countenance* in the quarter where the nation might have looked for *ſupport*. We have not, however, *ſubmitted*. We have *ſuffered*. We are now precluded from the poſſibility of conteſting the legality of the fine impoſed on us, for the payment thereof has been enforced at the Treaſury, without paſſing through the orninary medium of the Revenue Side of the Exchequer, where we might have inſtituted a legal enquiry into the matter before the Barons of that Court, from whoſe deciſion there *can* be no appeal, or writ of error to the Houſe of Lords.

A variety of cauſes may be aſſigned for the diſcontented ſtillneſs which prevails: the landed intereſt forms a body very nearly of an ariſtocratic complexion; the commercial intereſt is involved in public and private embarraſſment; the manufacturers are without a ſufficiency of employment, and credit has ſcarcely an exiſtence. But, notwithſtanding the prevalence of this ſullen torpor, let us not deſpair of our Country.——Although manœuvres to fruſtrate public energy are various, hardy and ſucceſsful; nevertheleſs, a wanton ſacrafice of perſonal liberty, and a lawleſs plunder of private property, will not fail to make an impreſſion proportionate to their enormity. We lament the arbitrary intemperance which has determined very many valuable and opulent members of the community to emigrate. And although we exult in the exiſtence of a new World, in which Freedom is ſecured, and equal law duly adminiſtered to a Nation of Citizens; yet, in our opinion, we ſhould not abandon our Country to ſeek thoſe bleſſings in a foreign land, until we ſhall have exhauſted every conſtitutional effort to eſtabliſh them at home. In that great cauſe we are bound to *ſuffer* as well as to *act*, and from the performance of that duty we have not *ſhrunk*. In the infamy of our impriſonment we take pride, for we take pride in our cauſe.——A Selden has been caſt into a common priſon before us, and yet he ſurvived the deſpotiſm which violated the Law and oppreſſed his Country.

Edinburgh, October 28, 1793.

UNTO THE HON. SHERIFF OF EDINBURGH.

The PETITION of WILLIAM SCOT,

PROCURATOR FISCAL of COURT, for the public Intereſt.

HUMBLY SHEWETH,

THAT in the Months of November and December laſt, or thereby, a moſt dangerous ſpirit of Sedition made its appearance amongſt many of the Leidges in this Country, which was carried to a very great height; and meetings promoted and called at many different places for the avowed purpoſe of creating Diſturbances, and overturning the happy Conſtitution of this Country——In particular the promoters of theſe meetings and ſeditious purpoſes, procured and brought about what they were pleaſed to term A Convention of the Friends of the People at Edinburgh, ſometime in the beginning of December laſt, which ſat and deliberated upon their ſeditious purpoſes for ſeveral days, during which period, or recently prior thereto, Mr. Archibald Hamilton Rowan, of the kingdom of Ireland, deſigning himſelf Secretary to the Society of United Iriſhmen in Dublin, did, with a malevolent and wicked intention, and with a view to promote and forward the aforeſaid ſeditious purpoſes, tranſmit, or cauſe to be tranſmitted, to one or more of the Members of the ſaid Meeting, at Edinburgh, calling or ſtyling themſelves, the Convention of the Friends of the People, a printed paper of a moſt dangerous and ſeditious tendency, entitled, " Addreſs from the Society of " United Iriſhmen in Dublin, to the Delegates " for promoting a Reform in Scotland;" which paper, and the dangerous Sentiments therein contained, were recommended by him to that Meeting, and they urged in conſequence thereof to adopt the ſame.——That in the courſe of the months of June, July, or Auguſt laſt, the ſaid Archibald Hamilton Rowan, with the ſame wicked and malicious Intent, alſo ſent more of theſe printed papers, with other papers or pamphlets, of a ſeditious and dangerous tendency to the Conſtitution of theſe Kingdoms to Scotland, to be diſperſed and circulated there. And not ſatisfied with this, he, with the ſame malicious and wicked Intent, and for other ſeditious and dangerous purpoſes, is juſt now come to this Country, and is * within your Lordſhip's juriſdiction.—In order therefore, to check ſuch illegal and unwarrantable proceedings, and prevent the fatal conſequences which might enſue therefrom; as alſo that the ſaid Archibald Hamilton Rowan may be puniſhed according to Law if guilty; your Lordſhip's warrant to the effect after mentioned is craved.

* It is obſervable, that though this petition, and Warrant granted thereon, which bears date the 28th of October, 1793, ſtates Mr. Archibald Hamilton Rowan to be then within the juriſdiction of the Sheriff of Edinburgh; yet Mr. Archibald Hamilton Rowan did not leave Dublin until the evening of the 31ſt of the ſaid month,—arrived in Edinburgh at one o'clock of the 4th November, 1793; and in leſs than one hour afterwards he was taken into cuſtody.

May it therefore pleaſe your Lordſhip to grant Warrant to Officers of Court, and other executors of the Law, to ſearch for and apprehend the perſon of the ſaid Archibald Hamilton Rowan, wherever he can be found within this Shire, and to bring him before you for examination—and thereafter, if you ſee cauſe, to commit him priſoner to the Talbooth of Edinburgh, or Canongate, therein to remain until liberate in due courſe of Law, according to Juſtice.

(Signed) WILLIAM SCOT, P. F.

Edinburgh, October 28, 1793.

The Sheriff having conſidered this petition, grants Warrant to Officers of Court to apprehend and bring before him the perſon of the within deſigned Archibald Hamilton Rowan, for examination.

(Signed) JOHN PRINGLE.

November 4, 1793.

The which day, compeared in the preſence of John Pringle, Eſq. Advocate, his Majeſty's Sheriff Depute of the Shire of Edinburgh, Archibald Hamilton Rowan, Eſq. of Rathcoffy, in the County of Kildare, Ireland, who being examined * and interrogated, Whether or not

* This examination was carried on in ſecret; the Sheriff Depute, the Sheriff's ſubſtitute, two Clerks, the Procurator Fiſcal, the Meſſenger, and Mr. Archibald Hamilton Rowan, were the only perſons preſent.—Mr. Archibald Hamilton Rowan requeſted that Mr. Butler ſhould be admitted, but his requeſt was refuſed, it being contrary to the cuſtoms and laws of Scotland, to admit at ſuch examination the preſence of any perſon on behalf of the party under examination.

the Declarant is acquainted with Mr. Thomas Muir, younger, of Hunter's-Hill, presently prisoner in the Talbooth of Edinburgh, declares, That had the Declarant been in his own Country when he was apprehended, he would have requested to see the Warrant, but thinking the first duty of a good Citizen, to be submission to authority, and appeal to the Law for Redress, he has attended; but being ignorant of the Laws of this Country, and not knowing how far he may criminate himself, and thinking the interrogatory unconstitutional in itself, he begs leave to decline answering.——Interrogated—Did the Declarant in the months of November, December, or January last, transmit, or cause to be transmitted, to the said Thomas Muir, or to any other person in Scotland a printed paper, dated November 23d, 1792, entitled, "Address from "the Society of United Irishmen in Dublin, to "the Delegates for promoting a Reform in "Scotland, William Drennan, Chairman, Archi-"bald Hamilton Rowan, Secretary; declares, That for the reasons above mentioned, and because the Declarant, sees that the accusations against him, are the having transmitted such an address, he declines answering.——Interrogated—Did the Declarant write a Letter to the said Mr. Muir, or any other person, desiring him to lay the aforesaid address, before the meeting of Delegates for promoting a Reform in Scotland, designing themselves the Convention of the Friends of the People in Scotland? Declares and declines answering for the reasons already assigned.——Interrogated.—Did the Declarant see the aforesaid Mr. Muir in Ireland, in the months of June, July, or August last, and then give Mr. Muir a copy, or copies of a printed Pamphlet, entitled, "Proceedings of the Society of United

" Irishmen in Dublin?" Declares, That the Declarant conceives the whole of this examination, as tending to criminate himself; that he is not conscious of having ever acted unlike a good Citizen, either here or in his own Country, and appeals to the justice of his cause, when legally and constitutionally brought forward, for his exculpation, declining to answer the question. ——Interrogated—At what time the Declarant arrived in Edinburgh? Declares, That he arrived about one o'clock in the afternoon of this Day. ———Interrogated—Has the Declarant seen or spoke with the aforesaid Mr. Muir, since the Declarant arrived in Edinburgh? Declares, That the Messenger who took him into custody, found him in Mr. Muir's room.———Interrogated—Did the Declarant come to Edinburgh at present, as a Delegate from Ireland, to attend the Convention of the Friends of the People at Edinburgh? Declares, That if he had the honour of being appointed as a Delegate to attend that Meeting he would have taken care to come before it had broke up.——Interrogated, Did the Declarant write a Letter to any person in this Country, intimating that he meant to attend the aforesaid Meeting as a Delegate from Ireland, or in any other capacity? Declares that he did not. ——Interrogated—Did the Declarant receive an invitation from any person or persons in this Country, to attend a Meeting, designing themselves a Convention of the *Friends of the People*, and which was held in Edinburgh last week? Declares, *That he did not receive such invitation*. ——Interrogated—Did the Declarent receive an invitation to attend any other Meeting for Reform in Edinburgh, under any other designation than that above mentioned? Declares, That *he received no invitation to attend any Meeting whatever, in Edinburgh.* Declares and acknowledges, That the petition of the Procurator Fiscal, with the Sheriff's Warrant upon it, in consequence of which the Declarant was apprehended and brought before the Sheriff, was read over to the Declarant before the examination proceeded. All this he declares to be truth.

(Signed)
ARCHIBALD HAMILTON ROWAN.
JOHN PRINGLE.

The before designed Archibald Hamilton Rowan, being further examined, and shewn a printed Pamphlet, entitled, "Proceedings of the Society of United Irishmen in Dublin," and Interrogated, Whether the Declarant has before seen the said Pamphlet, or any copy of it? Declares that he knows, that the Society of United Irishmen published their proceedings, but does not know whether the copy now shewn him, be a copy of their proceedings or not.——Interrogated—Whether or not the Declarant, at any time, acted in the capacity of Secretary to any of the Meetings of the aforesaid Society United Irishmen? Declares and declines answering this question, for the reasons already assigned. Being Interrogated, and desired to consider the Pamphlet now shewn to him, and to say to the best of his knowledge and belief, whether or not it is the publication made by the above mentioned Society, as before declared to? Declares and declines answering the question; and which Pamphlet is marked as relative hereto of this date. All this he also declares to be truth.

(Signed)
ARCHIBALD HAMILTON ROWAN.
JOHN PRINGLE.

The before written Declaration, consisting of the ten preceding pages, was freely and voluntarily emitted Mr. Archibald Hamilton Rowan, therein designed, in presence of John Pringle, Esq. Advocate Sheriff Depute of the shire of Edinburgh; Harry Davedson, Esq. Sheriff Substitute, and Mr. William Scot, Procurator Fiscal of said shire; George Williamson, Messenger, in Edinburgh; Joseph Mack, and James Williamson, Writers in Edinburgh. The Declaration being wrote by the said Joseph Mack.

(Signed) HARRY DAVEDSON.
WILLIAM SCOT.
JOSEPH MACK.
GEORGE WILLIAMSON.
JAM. WILLIAMSON.

November 4, 1793.

The Petitioner represents, that as the within designed Archibald Hamilton Rowan, Esq. when under examination before your Lordship, declined to answer several questions put to him. The Petitioner is entitled to have your Lordship's Warrant against Mr. Archibald Hamilton Rowan, to commit him for further examination. But as the enquiries and further examinations may take up a considerable time, and thereby lay Mr. Archibald Hamilton Rowan under confinement, the Petitioner shall consent that he be liberated from the present, upon finding caution to stand Tryal, in any criminal complaint to be brought against him, for the crimes charged in the petition, and craves that your Lordship will grant Warrant accordingly.

(Signed) WILLIAM SCOT.

Edinburgh, November 3, 1793.

The Sheriff having refumed the confideration of this petition, declaration of the within defigned Archibald Hamilton Rowan, taken before him of this date, with the before written minute, grants Warrant to Officers of Court, and George Williamfon, Meffenger at Arms, to apprehend, and incarcerate him in the Tolbooths of Edinburgh, or Canongate; the Keepers whereof are hereby ordered to receive and detain him, ay and until he find caution acted in the Sheriff Court Books of Edinburgh, to anfwer to abide Tryal, and underlye the Law, in any complaint or criminal profecution to be brought againft him, within the fpace of fix Months, from the date of fuch caution, before any Court competent upon the fubject matter of this petition, and that under the penalty of three thoufand Marks, Scots Money.

(Signed) JOHN PRINGLE.

At Edinburgh, the fourth Day of November, feventeen hundred and ninety-three years.

The which Day compeared, Colonel Norman Mc. Leod, refiding in George's-Street, Edinburgh, and judicially enacts, binds, and obliges himfelf, his heirs, executors, and fucceffors, as cautioners and furetys, acted in the Sheriff Court Books of Edinburgh, for Archibald Hamilton Rowan, Efq. of the kingdom of Ireland, prefently in Edinburgh, that he fhall prefent the perfon of the faid Archibald Hamilton Rowan, Efq. at any time and place to which he fhall be lawfully fummoned, within the fpace of fix Months from this date, and at all the after dyets of Court, to anfwer to abide Tryal, and underlye the Law in any in any complaint, or criminal proſecution to be brought againſt him, within the ſpace aforeſaid, before any Court competent, either at the inſtance of his Majeſty's Advocate, or the Procurator Fiſcal of Court, upon the ſubject matter of the petition and information preſented to the Sheriff of Edinburgh, whereon the warrant of commitment againſt him did of this date proceed, and that under the penalty of three thouſand Marks, Scots Money.

(Signed) NORMAN Mc. LEOD.

At Edinburgh, the fourth Day of November, ſeventeen hundred and ninety-three years,

What is wrote upon this, and the preceding pages, is a juſt copy of the Proceedings before the Sheriff of Edinburgh, reſpecting Archibald Hamilton Rowan, Eſq.

JOSEPH MACK.

The following is the copy of a Letter from ARCHIBALD HAMILTON ROWAN, Esq; to the Sheriff of Edinburgh, dated November 6th, 1793, which is to be held as part of the declaration.

JOSEPH MACK.

MY LORD,

IN consequence of your kind permission of this morning, I trouble you with the following explanation: Upon reading over the Interrogatory, and examining my papers, I find an incorrectness might be implied from two of the answers I gave to you in my examination, which I beg leave to elucidate.

"Interrogated—Did the Declarant receive an "invitation from any person or persons in this "Country, to attend a Meeting, designing them-"selves a Convention of the *Friends of the Peo-"ple*, and which was held in Edinburgh last "week? Declares that he did not receive such "invitation.——Interrogated—Did the Decla-"rant receive an invitation to attend any other "Meeting for Reform in Edinburgh, under any "other designation, than that above mentioned? "Declares that he received no invitation to at-"tend any Meeting whatever in Edinburgh."

Now I do find that I did receive a Letter in Ireland from an Individual, which contained the following paragraph:—"I could most earnestly "wish that you, or any of your friends, would "without delay, do us the honour of a visit."

I did not recollect this paragraph when I was brought before you, I hardly think it can be called an invitation, I certainly did not think it ſuch; and I declare upon my honour, that that Letter was not the occaſion of my coming to Scotland.

I am, my Lord, &c.

(Signed)

ARCHIBALD HAMILTON ROWAN.

N. B. Norman Mc. Leod, Eſq; who became the bail of Mr. Archibald Hamilton Rowan, is Member of Parliament for Invernefsſhire; a Gentleman of large property and extenſive connexions. The circumſtances of this buſineſs being reported to him, while Mr. Archibald Hamilton Rowan was under examination, he attended at the Sheriff's Court, and although he was an entire ſtranger to Mr. Archibald Hamilton Rowan, yet he inſiſted in the handſomeſt manner on becoming bound as his bail.

Friday, November 22d, 1793,

THE SOCIETY OF UNITED IRISHMEN

IN DUBLIN,

TO MR. THOMAS MUIR.

WE who so lately heard you, in the centre of our circle, pour out, with a fervour of rational declamation, the earnest prayer of an honest heart, for the freedom, peace and happiness of the human race, have felt, as men ought to feel, (for you are now every man's countryman) on hearing an account, from eye-witnesses, of your present rigorous imprisonment preparatory to fourteen years; not of banishment, but of transportation from your native land,——for what?—for conspiring against the Corruptions of the Constitution, and zealously striving to give a representation to two millions and a half of people.—We address you in no strain of ideot ceremony, but as men sympathising with man suffering; the language alive and the heart affected.

Let the few Lawyers who can look down on their profession from the height of their nature, expatiate with a noble indignation on the consequence of "Politics entering into the Courts of Justice and seating herself on the Bench," sharpening the severity of sentence with the snappishness of office, and the acrimony of personal vengeance, seizing with greediness the advantage of unascertained and uncertain punishment, rioting upon *Discretion*, and without weighing the intrinsic nature of the offence or the inadequacy of the penalty, really punishing Public Opinion, and accumulating all the exasperation felt against the prevailing ſenſe of the community, on the head of an unhappy individual. Let thoſe ſingular Lawyers detail with energy the terrible defects of judicial procedure in Scotland, through all its ſtages from accuſation to conviction. Let them inſtance thoſe particular irregularities in form which have vitiated your trial, in the opinion of the beſt lawyers, as it has already been deemed vitiated by its vindictive ſpirit, in the minds of the beſt men. Let this be done—but this is too technical a taſk for our feelings, nor does it indeed correſpond to the dignity, we will venture to call it, the proud importance of your preſent ſtation. We ſpeak to you as Citizens to a Friend and Brother, Citizens condenſed together in affection, perhaps the more from the frozen indifference, which, for the preſent, we feel around us.

You ought then, Dear Aſſociate! you ought to extract comfort from your preſent ſituation. Pleaſure often ſickens, but there is ſublime and permanent delight in ſtruggling with unmerited misfortune. The cabinet contains its ſufferings, its doubts and its deſpondence; the cell has its enjoyments, its hopes, and the nightly viſitation of ſelf-approving conſcience. Has it not already ſhown you, auſterely but truely, the diſtinction between what is laſting and what is periſhable? Has it not winnowed the world for your uſe, and ſeparated the chaff of mankind from the grain? Do you not now feel the value of that friendſhip which clings to the forſaken, the value of that ſimple and ſincere prayer which the poor of Scotland are daily offering up for the Advocate of the People, expelled from his profeſſion, becauſe his principles were not thoſe of a Craft, and baniſhed from his country for having thought as Blackſtone, as Locke, and as Sidney? Is it not ſweet to think that every hour you now live is *productive*, that your life is not wasted, but burns away an offering on the altar of humanity; that your example serves to inspirit others in the same situation; that your solid virtue may have been the means of averting from others, the sufferings you yourself experience; and, that many who now enjoy their firesides, their wives, and their children may be indebted to your prompt interposition, your steady zeal and your patient magnanimity? Is it not sweet to thing that your confinement or exile may, in any way, tend to the liberty of others.

——If that can be called Liberty where the public soul is imprisoned, where suspicion clouds the open, candid front of man; where the amiable ingenuousness that keeps no guard, and in the simplicity of the heart forgets to place a seal on the lip, is, at every hour, and in every place, exposed to calumny that lies in silent watch, with all the venom of the snake, and without its rattle.—If that can be called Public Liberty, where two men meet, and after eying each other askance, *both* ask "What News?" because neither dare answer the question; where the morality of a man may be spotless and yet his person be proscribed and his principles accounted pestilential.—If that can be called Public Liberty, where at the once social table, we see feast without fellowship, company without cordiality, and the jingle of frigid glasses without a free interchange of sentiment, and a mixture of mind—Where at the still dearer domestic board, the wife shudders, when her husband drops a word on the strange impressive scenes that are passing before mens eyes, and in a panic, sends off the attendants for fear they have glided into the family as spies, and removes her very children lest they should hear their honest parent give vent to the bitterness of his heart, and call down a curse on the men who have been curses to their country.

Alas for that Country! alas for that Conſtitution, ſet in ſuch hideous forms before the eyes of thoſe who *wiſh* to love it, and guard it, and ſave it from a conflagration that threatens to involve every thing human and divine?—That our rulers would or could *think at large!*—That they would not fit their minds merely to the dimenſions of their cloſets, and their plans to the expedients of an hour?—That they would go abroad and aſcend to ſuch a mental elevation, as not only to contemplate the murmuring multitude below, but with a preſcience derived from recollection, to command a proſpect into futurity, to trace the progreſs of mind through the lapſe of ages, till loſt in Eternal Truth, ſtill flowing onward, ſtill enlarging, riſing over every obſtacle and ſometimes ſmooth, deep and ſilent, juſt before it breaks down into a cataract, followed by a tide wild, broken and innavigable, Would to God, that, inſtead of puniſhing a worthy man for mixing with the commonalty, our rulers would not merely connive at, but encourage ſuch an approximation and intimacy between higher and lower ſociety as would cure the vices incident to each, bring the one *down* and the other *up* to their nature, humanizing the great, ennobling the vulgar, and tempering the ferocity of both, in ſhort, as would, by turning uſeleſs pyramids of Power into humble and chearful Habitations, make man reliſh his ſituation and deprecate all change as the worſt of misfortunes!

In whatever part of the world, Dear Sir, it may be your deſtiny to dwell, believe us, you will hear along with you our reſpect, our affection, our admiration. There is an electricity that at preſent pervades the univerſal mind, and were you placed at the extremity of the globe, the heart of every

Patriot will always feel the Touch of *your* Condition; we ſeel much at preſent on hearing of your illneſs; we hope there are many years before you; but if otherwiſe, be ſatisfied, for you have not lived in vain. If death be, as we believe it, but a pauſe in exiſtence, your happineſs is yet to come; and if death be, as we truſt in God it is *not*, an eternal *ſleep*, are not the dreams of ſuch an honeſt man infinitely preferable to the perpetual incubus of a guilty conſcience?

Edinburgh, Monday November 25th, 1793.

THE BRITISH CONVENTION.

OF the Delegates of the People, aſſociated to obtain Univerſal Suffrage and Annual Parliaments, after taking into their Conſideration the oppreſſed State of their Brethren in Ireland, and the Unconſtitutional Act of the laſt Seſſion of their Parliament called *The Convention Act*; and ſeeing with Indignation, that by that Act they were deprived of thoſe Rights, cheaply purchaſed by the Blood of our common Anceſtors, and which have ſince been confirmed and ſecured by the great Charter of our Liberties:

RESOLVED, *That all, or any of the Patriotic Members of the Society of* UNITED IRISHMEN *of* DUBLIN, *ſhall be admitted to ſpeak and vote in this* CONVENTION,

RESOLVED, *That the above Reſolution be tranſmitted to Citizen* HAMILTON ROWAN, *to be by him communicated to the* UNITED IRISHMEN *of* DUBLIN.

Signed by Order of the Convention,
MAT. CAMPELL BROWNE, *Preſident*.
W. SKIRVING, *Secretary*.

SOCIETY OF UNITED IRISHMEN OF DUBLIN, TO THE BRITISH CONVENTION.

YOUR resolution in favour of this Society has been communicated to us by our highly respected ARCHIBALD HAMILTON ROWAN.

If Irishmen now consult, through the medium of Delegation (the best mode of avoiding tumult and obtaining cool deliberation) on the means of procuring a Representation of the Nation in the House of Commons, they become feloniously criminal: We therefore receive your resolution, not as a debt due to our merits or our sufferings, but as a measure of manly and energetic policy, the only remaining means of union with Ireland. Those men who are interested in resisting the measures of Reform in the three Kingdoms, have long since conspired together, and have frequently experienced the benefits resulting from such co-operation: It is by that union they have been so long enabled to oppress the Democracy of these Countries. Identity of interest and object is their bond of union; let us learn wisdom from our enemies, and let us also be united by identity of interest and of object. Our repeated failures of success must convince us, that while each Nation stands back, waiting until the others shall have made the first struggle, we must all be baffled. Our cause is a common cause, and must be won by common exertions.

Certain measures, which have been recently taken in this Country to stifle the voice of the

People, may probably, in consequence of this wide extended conspiracy against Reform, be adopted in Great Britain with a similar intention. While yet unrestrained, guard against the impending danger; deliberate in time upon the means of frustrating the attempt, should it be made; and of avoiding its oppressive consequences, should it be successful: and if you can devise a mode by which we may all, in such case co-operate, you may rely on our exertions.

It is to inculcate this principle of union, and not with the idea of conferring honour, that we have passed the resolution we now inclose to you. By it you will find we have not only embraced all the Members of your Convention as Brothers and Associates, but have also extended those titles to all your Constituents. To them we request you will make known this assurance of our affection. Tell them it is at this moment of danger and persecution, while you are threatened with all the complicated miseries, a malignant policy, yet unglutted with the multitude of its victims, can inflict, that we are cemented together by the unity of our cause, and pledge ourselves to an undeviating fidelity for its success.

In pursuance of the great object of our Association, we are now preparing such a plan of Reform, as, in our apprehension, will, if carried into effect, give an impartial and adequate Representation to the People in Parliament. When arranged, it shall be transmitted either to you, if you should be then assembled, or otherwise to the several Societies by which you are Delegated.

A PLAN

OF AN EQUAL REPRESENTATION OF THE PEOPLE OF IRELAND IN THE HOUSE OF COMMONS.

Prepared for Public Consideration by the SOCIETY *of* UNITED IRISHMEN *of* DUBLIN.

I. THAT the Nation, for the Purpose of Representation solely, should be divided into 300 Electorates, formed by Combination of Parishes, and as nearly as possible equal in Point of Population.

II. THAT each Electorate should return one Representative to Parliament.

III. THAT each Electorate should, for the Convenience of carrying on the Elections at the same Time, be subdivided into a sufficient Number of Parts.

IV. THAT there should be a returning Officer for each Electorate, and a deputy returning Officer for each Subdivision, to be respectively elected.

V. THAT the Electors of the Electorate should vote, each in the Subdivision in which he is registered, and has resided as herein after specified.

VI. THAT the returning Officers of the Subdivisions should severally return their respective Polls to the returning Officer of the Electorate, who should tot up the Whole, and return the Person having a Majority of Votes, as the Representative in Parliament.

VII. THAT every Man poſſeſſing the Right of Suffrage for a Repreſentative in Parliament, ſhould exerciſe it in his own Perſon only.

VIII. THAT no Perſon ſhould have a Right to vote in more than one Electorate at the ſame Election.

IX. THAT every Male of ſound Mind, who has attained the full Age of 21 Years, and actually dwelt, or maintained a Family Eſtabliſhment in any Electorate for ſix Months of the Twelve immediately previous to the Commencement of the Election, (provided his Reſidence, or maintaining a Family Eſtabliſhment be duly regiſtered) ſhould be intitled to vote for the Repreſentative of the Electorate.

X. THAT there ſhould be a Regiſtering Officer, and a Regiſtry of Reſidence in every Subdiviſion of each Electorate; and that in all Queſtions concerning Reſidence, the Regiſtry ſhould be conſidered as concluſive Evidence.

XI. THAT all Elections in the Nation ſhould commence and cloſe on the ſame Day.

XII. THAT the Votes of all Electors ſhould be given by Voice and not by Ballot.

XIII. THAT no Oath of any Kind ſhould be taken by any Elector.

XIV. THAT the full Age of 25 Years ſhould be a neceſſary Qualification to intitle any Man to be a Repreſentative.

XV. THAT Reſidence within the Electorate ſhould not, but that Reſidence within the Kingdom ſhould be a neceſſary Qualification for a Repreſentative.

XVI. THAT no Property Qualification ſhould be neceſſary to intitle any Man to be a Repreſentative.

XVII. That any Perſon having a Penſion, or holding a Place in the Executive or Judicial Departments, ſhould be thereby diſqualified from being a Repreſentative.

XVIII. That Repreſentatives ſhould receive a reaſonable Stipend for their Services.

XIX. That every repreſentative ſhould, on taking his Seat, ſwear that neither he, nor any Perſon to promote his Intereſt, with his Privity, gave or was to give any Bribe for the Suffrage of any Voter.

XX. That any Repreſentative convicted by a Jury, of having acted contrary to the Subſtance of the above Oath, ſhould be for ever diſqualified from ſitting or voting in Parliament.

XXI. That Parliaments ſhould be Annual.

XXII. That a Repreſentative ſhould be at Liberty to reſign his Delegation upon giving ſufficient Notice to his Conſtituents.

XXIII. That Abſence from Duty for
ſhould vacate the Seat of a Repreſentative.

THE SOCIETY OF UNITED IRISHMEN OF

DUBLIN

TO THE PEOPLE OF IRELAND.

PEOPLE OF IRELAND,

WE new submit to your cosideration, a plan for your equal representation in the House of Commons. In framing it, we have disregarded the many over-charged accusations, which we hear daily made by the prejudiced and the corrupt, against the People, their independence, integrity and understanding. We are, ourselves, *but a portion of the People*; and that appellation, we feel, confers more real honour and importance, than can, in *these times*, be derived from Places, Pensions, or Titles. As little have we consulted the sentiments of Administration or of Opposition. We have attentively observed them both, and, whatever we may hope of some members of the latter, we firmly believe that both those parties are equally averse from the measure of adequate reform. If we had no other reason for that opinion, the plan laid before Parliament, in the last session, under the auspices of Opposition, might convince us of the melancholy truth. Thus circumstanced, then, distrusting all Parties, we hold it the right and the duty of every Man in the Nation, to examine, deliberate, and decide for himself on that important measure. *As a portion of the People* (for in no other capacity, we again repeat it, do we presume to address you) we suggest to you our ideas, by which we would provide to preserve the popular part of the Legislature uninfluenced by, and independent of the other two parts, and to effectuate that essential principle of justice and of our Constitution, that every Man has the right of voting, thro' the medium of his representative, for the law by which he is bound: that sacred principle, for which America fought, and by which Ireland was emancipated from British supremacy! If our ideas are right, which we feel an honest conviction they are, adopt them, if wrong, discussion will detect their errors, and *we at least*, shall be always found ready to profit by, and conform ourselves to the sentiments of the People.

Our present state of representation is charged with being unequal, unjust, and by no means calculated to express *your* deliberate will, on any subject of general importance. We have endeavoured to point out the remedies of those evils, by a more equal distribution of political power and liberty; *by doing justice*; and by anxiously providing that your deliberate will shall be, at all times, accurately expressed in your own Branch of the Legislature. If these are not the principles of good government, we have yet to learn from the Placemen and Pensioners that flit about the Castle, in what the science of Politics can consist. But we know they are, and we are bold to say, that the more a government carries these principles into effect, the nearer it approaches to perfection.

We believe it will be said that our plan, however just, is impracticable in the present state of this Country. If any part of that impracticability should be supposed to result from the interested resistance of borough-proprietors, although we never will consent to compromise the *Public*

Right, yet we, for our parts, might not hesitate to purchase the *Public Peace* by an adequate compensation. At all events, it rests with you, Countrymen, not with us, to remove the objection. If you do not wish the accomplishment of such a Reform, it will not take place: if you do, we cannot believe that Ireland is *yet* sunk to that state of mis-government, in which it may be truly said, that although the great body of the People seriously feel the justice of a measure, and are seriously determined on its attainment, it is nevertheless impracticable.

To you, among our Countrymen, for whose welfare we have peculiarly laboured from the first moment of our institution, and the contemplation of whose prosperity will more than compensate us for the sufferings we may have endured, for the calumnies with which we are aspersed, and for those which the publication of this unpalateable plan will call down upon us; *To you the poorer classes of the Community* we now address ourselves. We are told you are ignorant; we wish you to enjoy Liberty, without which no People was ever enlightened: we are told you are uneducated and immoral; we wish you to be educated, and your morality improved, by the most rapid of all instructors—a good government. Do you find yourselves sunk in poverty and wretchedness? Are you overloaded with burdens, you are but little able to bear? Do you feel many grievances, which it would be tedious, and might be *unsafe* to mention? Believe us, they can all be redressed by such a reform as will give *you* your just proportion of influence in the Legislature, AND BY SUCH A MEASURE ONLY. To that, therefore, we wish to rivet all your attention. Let those Men, who wrangle about preserving or acquiring power, catch at popularity by their petty regulations to check the progreſs of theſe growing evils; do you deliberate, in the retirement of your hearts, upon their only adequate remedy. Deſiſt, we entreat you, from thoſe diſturbances, which are a diſgrace to your Country, and an injury to yourſelves, which impair your own ſtrength, and impede your own cauſe. Examine, *peaceably and attentively*, the plan of reform we now ſubmit to you. Conſider, *Does it propoſe to do* YOU *juſtice? Does it propoſe to give* YOU *ſufficient protection?* for we have no fears, but that the Rich will have juſtice done to them, and will be always ſufficiently protected. Hang this plan up in your Cabbins: think on it over and over again: Do not throw it by in deſpair, as being impoſſible to be carried into effect; FOR NOTHING, WE HOPE, IS IMPOSSIBLE THAT IS JUST.

February 7th, 1794.

THE SOCIETY OF UNITED IRISHMEN OF

DUBLIN,

TO ARCHIBALD HAMILTON ROWAN, Esq,

WE offer you our congratulations the only testimonial of our regard, which could be acceptable to you. We disdain to address a mind like yours in the language of pity and condolence. Although torn from what constituted the chief felicity of your being, the Society of an amiable exemplary wife, and the superintendance of a numerous and promising offspring, you are plunged into a loathsome prison. Yet the rectitude of your cause, the firmness of your principles, the unbending energy of your mind, the ardent affection of your grateful Countrymen, (to the assertion of whose liberties you have devoted yourself) will chear and sustain you through the progress of a tedious imprisonment.

When we call to recollection, the illustrious dead who stood forward, the champions and victims of their Country's cause.—When we think of Hambden, of Russel and of Sidney, who have sealed their principles with their blood, all inferior feelings subside and we forget the severity of your sufferings in their glory.

Although corruption has been leagued with falsehood, to misrepresent and vilify this Society, we have reposed in honest confidence on the consoling reflection, that we should at all times find an impregnable barrier in the TRIAL BY JURY—Wherein *character* and *intention* should be regarded as unerring guides to juſtice. But while we have been earneſtly endeavouring to eſtabliſh the conſtitutional rights of our Country, we ſuddenly find ourſelves at a loſs for this FIRST AND LAST STAKE OF A FREE PEOPLE, for the trial by Jury, loſes its whole value, when the Sheriff or the Pannell, are under the influence of intereſt, prejudice or deluſion, and that battery which liberty and wiſdom had united to conſtruct for the ſecurity of the People, is turned againſt them.

However in defiance of that ſyſtem of proſcription, which is no longer confined to a particular perſuaſion, but which viſits with vengeance every exertion in the cauſe of freedom, we truſt you are aſſured of our inflexible determination, to purſue the great object of our aſſociation.—An EQUAL AND IMPARTIAL REPRESENTATION OF THE PEOPLE IN PARLIAMENT. An object from which no chance or change, no ſlander, no perſecution, no oppreſſion ſhall deter us.

Newgate, February 8th, 1794.

UNITED IRISHMEN,

YOU have greatly over-rated both my merits and my ſufferings. My merits, as a Citizen, conſiſt in an honeſt, and reſolute attachment, in my principles, and in my practice, to that bond of our Society, an Equal Repreſentation of the People in Parliament; which I conſider to be the eſſence of the Britiſh Conſtitution, and which I eſteem of abſolute neceſſity for the peace and liberty of Ireland.

Do not tarniſh the memory of the illuſtrious dead by haſty compariſons with the living. If my ſufferings, ſlight as they are in compariſon with paſt and PRESENT examples, ſhall in any way contribute to our common object, I ſhall deem myſelf both honoured and rewarded.

ARCH. HAMILTON ROWAN.

FAIS CE QUE DOY, ARRIVE QUE POURRA.

PROCEEDINGS IN CERTAIN ACTIONS WHEREIN JAMES NAPPER TANDY, Esq. WAS PLAINTIFF, JOHN EARL OF WESTMORELAND, AND OTHERS DEFENDANTS.

Exchequer. Pleas side.

James N. Tandy Esq. Plaintiff, The Right Hon. John Fane Earl of Westmoreland of the Kingdom of Great Britain. Defendant.

ON Thursday the 21st of June 1792, a Subpœna from the Pleas side of the Court of Exchequer, was served on the Defendant at the suit of the Plaintiff, and the four days for appearance expired on Tuesday; on that day Mr. Attorney General obtained the following order.

Tuesday, 26th June, 1792.

James N. Tandy, Esq. against John Earl of Westmorland.

MR. Attorney General of counsel for his Excellency the Lord Lieutenant of Ireland, the defendant in this cause, moves to prohibit the issuing any attachment against him, and to quash the Subpœna which issued in this cause; whereupon it is ordered by the Court, that Mr. Matthew Dowling, the plaintiffs attorney, do attend this Court at the sitting thereof to-morrow, and that no Process do issue against the said Defendant in the mean time.

KEMMIS.

CLONMELL.

On Wednesday the 27th of June Mr. Dowling attended the Court in obedience to the above Order, was ordered on the Table, and being asked by the Court if he had issued the Subpœna against the defendant, he admitted he had, and that the defendant was served with it—He was then asked by the Court to declare what the cause of action was—(Here the Hon. Simon Butler, one of Mr. Tandy's counsel, interfered, and protested against the question, and insisted that the attorney was not to disclose the secrets of his client, and that an attempt to sift him for that purpose was contrary to law and Justice). The Court then asked Mr. Dowling whether *he* had any objection to answer the question.—Mr. Butler again interfered and said, that as counsel for Mr. Tandy, he was indifferent whether *Mr. Dowling* had or had not any objection to answer the question, that it was sufficient that the *Client* had an objection, and that the privilege of the *Attorney* was the privilege of the *Client*, and he again pro-protested again the question. The court however thought proper to put the question, and Mr. Dowling peremptorily refused to disclose the cause of action. The court not thinking proper to press the question further, Mr. Dowling was dismissed without any other interrogatory.

Mr. Butler thereupon submitted to the court, that the motion of the Attorney General ought to be refused. He argued (in which particular he was strongly seconded by Mr. Mc. Nally) that the defendant not having entered an appearance, no motion on his behalf could be made; that there was in fact no cause in court but merely the *Institution* of a cause by process —Mr. Butler further contended that the proceedings in this case were instituted against the Earl of Westmorland of the kingdom of Great Britain, and that no document whatever had been adduced which could give the court judicial knowledge that the defendant was Lord Lieutenant of Ireland—the Attorney General had yesterday come into court with a piece of written paper in his hand, which he alledged was the copy of a Subpœna directed to the Right Hon. John Fane Earl of Westmoreland of the kingdom of Great Britain, and, upon an allegation that the Lord Lieutenant is not liable to any action, grounds a motion, that the Subpœna in this case be quashed or the proceedings stopt—but how did it come officially before the court to know the Lord Lieutenant was the person mentioned in the Subpœna? certainly not by any document or proof competent to warrant a compliance with the motion of the Attorney General. It was necessary that the Earl of Westmoreland should appear, and, on being declared against, plead that he is the Lord Lieutenant, and shew his letters patent in proof of the fact, before it can be considered as judicially before the Court.—Suppose the Earl of Westmoreland should come forward to shew his official qualification by his letters patent were without a seal, or otherwise defective in the forms which constituted their legality.—Suppose the Chief Justice of the King's Bench sued merely as Lord Clonmell, the court were not to know him as Chief Justice of the King's Bench, until he first came into court and pleaded and proved that he was so. The court had not in this case a competent judicial knowledge that the defendant was Lord Lieutenant—a judicial knowledge to be competent, must be founded on regular proof of the fact.

Hereupon the court declared that they had judicial knowledge that the defendant was Lord Lieutenant—it would be ridiculous for any man to pretend ignorance of it; they attended his summons to parliament in a judicial capacity; they saw him acting there in the capacity of Lord Lieutenant—they saw him attended with the usual state, and received in all the official dignities of Lord Lieutenant; therefore it was sufficient to announce to their official knowledge that he was Lord Lieutenant *de facto*, and they had nothing to do with the speculations *de jure*; that they had too full a knowledge of the British Constitution, to suppose there were two Earls of Westmoreland of the kingdom of Great Britain, or two peers titled of the same place—that they had besides the evidence of every sense that conveyed information to their mind, and would not, in complaisance to systems of special pleading, be prevailed on to affect a blindness to the evidence of their own senses, to that notoriety which must be impressed on the mind of every man in the kingdom who ever confidered the fubject for a moment.

Mr. Butler contended, that the court, in deciding the point in the prefent ftage, difpofed of a matter by way of *Order*, (from which no writ of error lies) which ought not to be difpofed of otherwife than by *Judgment*. If the Defendant appeared and pleaded, the Plaintiff might demur, and from the judgment of the court on the point the party is entitled to his writ of error, and thereby may obtain the decifion of the *dernier refort*; though the Lord Lieutenant figns the writ of error, he does fo minifterially merely, and not judicially, as the writ of error in civil cafes is *ex debito juftitia*, and not *ex gratia*; and therefore Mr. Butler firmly relied on his opinion as to the neceffity of Lord Weftmoreland's pleading in Court, and exhibiting documental proof of his being Lord Lieutenant, and begged permiffion to fay, that the court could not fee, hear, nor underftand judicially, that the Lord Lieutenant was the perfon meant, until the defendant appeared and pleaded that he was.

The court faid no man could be heard on this point, as they had delivered their opinions.

Mr. Butler obferved, that their Lordfhips had now given their decifion upon a point of the very utmoft importance, and upon grounds for which he knew no precedent.—But he had in his poffeffion an attefted Copy of the Letters Patent appointing the Earl of Weftmoreland Lord Lieutenant of Ireland.—By this document it appeared that his official rank as Lord Lieutenant of Ireland was conferred by Letters Patent under the *Great Seal of Great Britain*, and Mr. Butler did not hefitate to declare, that an official rank, *merely fo conftituted*, could not be recognized or have any weight in judicial decifion of any law court in this Independent kingdom. The Great Seal of Great Britain, in itself, has no more authority in this country than a mere cake of wax, or the Great Seal of the Mogul. The enrollment of it is an enrollment of a nullity, the Great Seal of Ireland was the only public instrument of authority that this country could acknowledge,—in this country the constitution of Ireland only could be acknowledged, and he knew of no constitution that should have weight or consideration in this court, but the constitution of Imperial and Independent Ireland; whether its principles were similar to, or taken from the British constitution was not for him to consider.

Court Would you, Mr. Butler, be understood to insinuate that there is no legal Chief Governor in this kingdom?

Mr. Butler, My Lords, the regard I have for the peace of this kingdom obliges me to decline an answer to your Lordships question, but the conclusion can be readily drawn from the premises.

Mr. Butler then argued that suppose the Defendant was considered as Lord Lieutenant, it does not necessarily follow that he in this case sued for an act done as Lord Lieutenant; the action may, for what the court know to the contrary, be brought against him in his private capacity.

The Chief Baron said that he in particular had judicial knowledge that the action was brought against the Defendant as Lord Lieutenant, because he was in the vacation applied to by the attorney for the plaintiff, to sign a letter missive addressed to the Earl of Westmoreland, Lord Lieutenant of Ireland.

Hereupon Mr. Dowling assured his Lordship that such address must have arisen from the mistake of the officer of the court, and was contrary to *his* directions.

Mr. Butler argued, that the addreſs of the letter miſſive would, in caſe it had been ſigned and proceedings had upon it, have been evidence merely to ſhew that the Earl of Weſtmoreland mentioned in that Letter Miſſive was Lord Lieutenant, but certainly would not have been evidence that the Defendant was ſued as for an act done by him as Lord Lieutenant; but that Letter Miſſive, not having been ſigned or proceeded upon, is out of the queſtion, and cannot be adduced as judicial knowledge of any fact in this caſe.

Mr. Butler then ſaid, that the queſtion for the opinion of the Court was, "whether any action civil or criminal can lie againſt a Lord Lieutenant of Ireland pending his Viceroyalty ?" a Doctrine is attempted to be ſet up that "no Civil or Criminal action will *locally* lie againſt a lord lieutenant *during his Government*"—If this Doctrine be true, the Current of Juſtice will be impeded, and the Rights of the ſubject will be in danger, for it can be made appear moſt evidently that no ſatisfaction can be obtained, either in this Kingdom or in any other, againſt a Lord Lieutenant *after* the end of his Goverement, for treſpaſſes committed by him during his Government. In every Caſe to repel the juriſdiction of the King's Courts, you muſt ſhew a more proper and a more ſufficient juriſdiction, for if there is no other mode of Trial, that alone will give the King's Courts a juriſdiction. Now, in this caſe, it is not ſhewn that an action could be ſuſtained at any other time in this Court or elſewhere—and Mr. Butler ſaid, that he would ſhew the negative, and demonſtrate to the Court, that after the diſſolution of the Government of a Lieutenant, an action could not, with effect, be maintained againſt him either in Ireland or elſewhere. Ireland is an independent Kingdom, and not, within the dominion of the Crown of Great Britain; an action of trespass, *vi & armis*, for a Trespass committed in Ireland, is not maintainable in great Britain, the Trespass was not committed *coctra pacem* of the King of Great Britain—so much for any chance of succeeding in an action in Great Britain. The case of Fabrigas and Mostin was the case of a Trespass committed in a place within the dominions of the Crown of Great Britain, and therefore an action for such Trespass was well maintainable in Westminster Hall. As to an action in this Kingdom at the end of the Viceroyalty, it is to be observed, that the Viceroy is a fugacious character, the subject of another Realm, to which he might return even before the dissolution of his authority; in his return to which he was guaranteed and protected even after the cessation of his authority here—where then was the chance of remedy or redress against him after he seceds or is dismissed from Office and returned into his country with his property? his authority is under the Great Seal of Great Britain; if not valid, he has no authority; if valid, the courts here are not competent to decide upon it—and the courts in Great Britain are not competent to take cognizance of a Trespass *vi & armis & contra pacem* committed in Ireland.—— The statute of limitations may also possibly have operations: in short, if the doctrine contended for was to hold, a Lord Lieutenant might commit any Trespass, might seize the property of the subject, imprison him, torture him, even Murder him with Impunity——Is the Court prepared to let such doctrine go abroad to the Irish Nation?

Mr. Butler was proceeding in his argument, and pressing the subject upon the Court—the Court declared, that they would give the most ample time for deliberation on all sides, and ordered the case to stand over till next Term, then to be fully argued.

Counsellor Emmet, for the plaintiff, moved that the Defendant do enter into security for his appearance at Court on the first day of next term—The Court refused the motion—the Attorney General declared that the Lord Lieutenant *would* not give security——Mr. Butler trusted that he *would*, if the Court was pleased to order him so to do.

Monday November 26th, 1792.

The motion being called on, Mr. Butler was directed by the Court to argue his Objections to the motion—Mr. Butler then submitted to the Court his reasons wherefore the Motion of the Attorney General should be refused—He said that the subpœna was issued at the suit of J. Napper Tandy Esq. against the Right Hon. John Fane Earl of Westmoreland of the Kingdom of Great Britain, and that, altho' until an appearance was entered, there was no cause in Court, and that, by the Rule of the Court, no motion could be made on behalf of any person who was not before the Court, yet Mr. Attorney General, alledging that the Defend. was the Lord Lieutenant, and that as such he was not liable to any action, moves that the subpœna be quashed or that no proceedings should issue upon it, and demands that the court will dispose of that by way of *order* (from which no writ of error lies)which ought not to be disposed of otherwise than by way of *judgment*. —The court having declared their judicial knowledge that the Defendant was Lord Lieutenant, and that the motion was not contrary to Lule, and that the matter might well be disposed of by way of order, Mr. Butler thereupon said that he would not trouble them further upon those points, but enter immediately upon the *general* queſtion, " whether any Civil or Criminal action will locally lie againſt a Lord Lieutenant during his Government", for he contended that the Court, not having before them any document whereon they could ground a judicial knowledge of the cauſe of action, could not know whether the writ was inſtituted againſt the Defend. for an act done by him in his *politic* or in his *natural* capacity, and were therefore compelled to decide the *general* queſtion.—He ſaid that the general Inviolability of a Lord Lieutenant from action (if any ſuch he has) muſt be grounded on his being, in quality of repreſentative of the King, the executive power of this country, aud if the inviolabilety extends to the Lord Lieutenant, it muſt alſo extend, by parity of reaſon, to a Lord Deputy and to Lords Juſtices.—It will be proper to conſider in what reſpect the king ſtands as to actions.—The original power of juriſdiction, by the fundamental principles of ſociety, is lodged in the ſociety as large: but every nation has committed that power to certain ſelect magiſtrates; and in England, this authority has been immemorially exerciſed by the King or his ſubſtitutes. However, in the times of our Saxon anceſtors, and even until the time of Edward the 1ſt, the King, tho' the reſervoir of Juſtice, might have been ſued in all actions as a common perſon, and for that purpoſe could iſſue a command to himſelf, the form of which was, " *Præcipe Henrica vegi Angliæ* &c."—1ſt. Comyn's Digeſt 104.—22d. Edw. 3d. 3—24th Edw. 3. 23. 55.—43 Edw. 3d. 22—Staunford's *Prærogativa Regis* 42.—Theloal's Dig. of original Writs Lib. 4. ch 1. S. 3.—(here the court having queſtioned the quotation, 1ſt. vol. Comyns's digeſt was produced, and they were then ſatisfied of its reality, obſerving only, that there was in Comyns a *dubitatur)*. It is true that at this day the mode of proceeding is otherwise, and that at this day the King cannot be sued as a common person may; for in some time after the conquest, when the fendal system introduced by the Norman Despots was established, the country ceased to be a nation and sunk into a kingdom, allodial and independant Tenures were abolished, the King became every thing, and the people nothing; the common law mode of suing the King became a matter of indecency, and it was thought improper that he should be subject to like process as a common person was; command, even by himself, became offensive to his organs of hearing, and in the Reign of the first Edward, who, tho' an able, was a despotic Prince, *petition* was established in its stead, and has ever since been continued as the mode; therefore at this day, if any person has, in point of *property*; a just demand upon the King, he must petition him in his Chancery, where his Chancellor will administer right as a matter of *grace* tho' not upon *compulsion*, for the end of such petition is not to *compel* the Prince to observe the contract, but to *persuade* him; but as to *personal wrongs*, as they are not to be presumed, if unfortunately they should happen to be committed, the subject is without remedy, for the inviolability of the Chief Magistrate is of more consequence than particular mischiefs.—This inviolability from action is however a direct and substantive and incommunicable prerogative, which the king has, in right of his royal dignity, over and above all other persons, and out of the ordinary course of the common law, and it is in its nature singular and eccentrical; the emphatical words of Magna Charta, spoken in the person of the King, who in judgment of Law is ever present and repeating them in all his Courts, are these, " *nulli vendemus. nulli negabimus aut differemus justitiam, vel rectam,*" and therefore "in every subject (says Lord Coke 2d. Inst. 55.) for injury done to him by any other subject, be he ecclesiastical or temporal without any exception, may take his remedy by the course of the Law and have justice and right for the injury done to him, freely without sale, fully without denial, and speedily without delay;" the law being the supreme arbiter of every man's life liberty and property, Courts of Justice must at all times be open to the subject, and the King cannot grant any exemption from suits, or communicate his prerogative in that respect to others. This prerogative, which gives the King inviolability from action, is besides in a great measure founded on his being the Reservoir from whence Justice is conducted, by a thousand channels, to every Individual; all jurisdictions of Courts are either mediately or immediately derived from him, their proceedings are generally in his name, they pass under his seal, and are executed by his officers; he has a legal ubiquity, he is always legally present in all his Courts, and the judges are the mirror by which his image is reflected.—But how can this reasoning be applied to a Lord Lieutenant; he is not the fountain of Justice, jurisdictions are not derived from him, their proceedings are not in his name, they pass not under his seal, and are not executed by his officers; he has no legal ubiquity, he is not legally present in all the Courts, and the Judges certainly are not the mirror by which his image is reflected. The act of the 21st. and 22d. Geo. 3d. Chap. 49. enacted in the year 1782, when we vainly flattered ourselves with the establishment of our Rights on a firm basis, does indeed make it lawful for a Lord Lieutenant to grant warrants for sealing writs of error returnable into Parliament; but surely this act, passed at ſuch a period, never was intended to operate for the Lord Lieutenant and inviolability from action; tho' the ſuitor muſt petition for the warrant, it will not be argued, that the Lord Lieutenant can refuſe to grant it, or that the granting or refuſing is a matter *ex gratia* and not *ex debito juſtitiæ*, or that the Lord Lieutenant, in granting it, acts otherwiſe than miniſterial.

Mr. Butler then argued, that if this Inviolability contended for on behalf of the Lord Lieutenant was allowed, it would not only be a delay, but a *denial* of Juſtice—In the caſe of the King, when the Law ſays that he ſhall not be ſued as a common perſon, it points out the petition as the mode of obtaining juſtice.—In order to repel one juriſdiction, another ſhould be ſhewn: but in the caſe of the Lord Lieutenant, no antidote is offered to the poiſon.—If he be privileged from action during the time of his Government, he never can be made reſponſible in this Kingdom for any act done during his Government, or in Great Britain for any Treſpaſs *vi et armis* he may commit here.—If he is privileged during his Government, he is privileged in his return home—the home of the Earl of Weſtmoreland is Great Britain, where he is a Peer and Privy Counſellor, and where conſequently the court will preſume that he will, in execution of his duty, reſide after the expiration of his Government; no proceſs therefore in this country can affect him perſonally, and any proceſs in this country againſt his property would be nugatory, he not having any property in this country upon which ſuch proceſs could attach. Suppoſe that after the expiration of his Government and departure from this Kingdom he ſhould return to it in a private capacity, and an action be inſtituted againſt him for an act done during his Government, and that he ſhould juſtify the act as having been done by virtue of his office of Lord Lieutenant, and make a profert of the letters patent appointing him Lord Lieutenant, If, upon oyer of thoſe letters patent, they ſhould appear to be under the Great Seal of Great Britain, does not the following dilemma preſent itſelf? He was either Lord Lieutenant or he was not; the patent was either legal or illegal; If he was not Lord Lieutenant, if the patent was illegal, he was not intitled to any privilege during his Government; if he was Lord Lieutenant, if the patent was legal, no action can be maintained againſt him in this Kingdom at any time for any act done during his Government, for he may juſtify any ſuch act under authority of ſuch letters patent, and the courts here are not competent to determine whether the act was warranted by ſuch authority or not, for the effect or extent of the letters patent of the King of Great Britain which gave the authority, can only be tried in the Courts of the King of Great Britain. In a word, the Earl of Weſtmoreland is either Lord Lieutenant by virtue of this patent, in which caſe no action can ever be maintained againſt him in this country for any act done during his Government, or he is not Lord Lieutenant by virtue of this Patent, in which caſe no perſon will contend that he has any privilege whatſoever.

Having endeavoured to ſhew, that ſuppoſing the Earl of Weſtmoreland to be Lord Lieutenant, and as ſuch privileged from action locally during his Government, he never can be made reſponſible in this Kingdom for any act done during his Government, Mr. Butler proceeded in his argument to ſhew, that he never can be made reſponſible in Great Britain for any treſpaſs *vi et armis* committed in this Kingdom.—There is a ſubſtantial diſtinction as to the *locality* of Trials with regard to matters that ariſe *out* of the Realm; there are ſome caſes that ariſe out of the Realm which ought not to be tried any where but in the country where they ariſe; an action of treſpaſs *vi et armis* for a treſpaſs *vi et armis* committed in Ireland is not maintainable in Great Britain, for, the breach of the Peace being merely local, though the treſpaſs againſt the perſon is tranſitory, it muſt be laid to be againſt the peace of the King, and the treſpaſs was not committed *contra pacem* of the King of Great Britain.—As to the caſe of General Moſtyn, and other caſes of Colonial Governors who were ſued after the expiration of their Governments in Weſtminſter Hall in actions of treſpaſs *vi et armis* for treſpaſſes committed in and during their Governments, they are not applicable to the caſe of a Lord Lieutenant of Ireland; they were the caſes of treſpaſſes committed in places within the dominions of the Crown of Great Britain, and therefore actions for ſuch treſpaſſes were well maintainable in Weſtminſter Hall; but Ireland is an independent kingdom and not within the dominions of the Crown of England, and therefore treſpaſſes *vi et armis* & *contra pacem* committed in Ireland are not cognizable by the courts in Weſtminſter Hall.—There is another difference very obſervable between a Lord Lieutenant of Ireland and Colonial Governors. The Lord Lieutenant preſides neither in a Court of equity nor of law; but the Governor has the cuſtody of the Great Seal, and is Chancellor within his province, with the ſame powers of judicature that the lord high Chancellor has in England; and the Governor preſides in the Court of errors, of which he and the council are Judges, to hear and determine all appeals in the nature of writs of error, from the ſuperior Courts of Common law in the Province —from whence it neceſſarily follows, that as a man ſhall not be Judge in his own cauſe, no action is maintainable againſt a Colonial Governor locally during his Government.—Stoke's on the conſtitution of the Britiſh colonies 185. —(Here the Court having denied the authority and declared that they never heard of the book or the author, Mr. Butler informed them that, the author was a Mr. Anthony Stoke's, a gentleman of the Inner Temple, a barriſter at law and formerly chief Juſtice of Georgia, and that his book was publiſhed in London, in 1783.) Mr. Butler further to ſhew that no action was maintainable in England, quoted the trial of Lord Strafford 1ſt ſtate trials 745, (the illegality of which is univerſally admitted) where that unfortunate Nobleman warmly and powerfully contended, that for any offence committed by him in Ireland, he was to be judged by the peers of Ireland.

Mr. Butler having endeavoured to ſhew, that no action would lie againſt Lord Weſtmoreland in Great Britain, and that if he was Lord Lieutenant and privileged while he was ſuch, no action could be afterwards maintained againſt him in this kingdom, proceeded in his argument, and expreſſed his apprehenſions, that even were an action maintainable againſt him in this kingdom after the expiration of his Government, he might plead the ſtatute of limitations in bar, and that the plaintiff could not reply that the defendant had during that period been Lord Lieutenant of Ireland; the ſtatutes give no ſuch replication; the caſe of a Chief Governor, is not provided for by any ſaving proviſo; the limitation clause has negative words, it enacts, that the actions therein specified shall be sued within the times therein mentioned and *not after*, and the saving provisoes make no mention of the case of a Chief Governor, and extend only to the particular circumstances and situation therein mentioned of a *plaintiff*, viz. minority, coverture, insanity, imprisonment, and absence beyond seas, and not to the circumstance or situation of a *defendant*, save only in one instance, viz. absence beyond seas.—

Mr. Butler said that he would conclude with one case of the very first authority, communicated to him by Mr. G. J. Browne, by which it would appear that in former times, and those not the most affected towards rights of the subject, very different ideas from the present were entertained of a Chief Governor's liability to be sued. In Lord Strafford's state letters, Vol. 1. p. 68, there is a letter from the Lord Justice to the Lord Deputy, dated the 26th. Feb. 1631 "There was a parish church commonly called "St. Andrew's church, situate in Dammes-"street in this city, which in former times of "disturbance here, by reason of the convenient "situation thereof near the castle was used for "a stable for the deputy's Horses; that Church "is now legally evicted from us in the Chancery "of his Majesty's court of Exchequer by the "Chapter of the Cathedral Church of St. Pa-"trick's Dublin to whom it belongs, and an in-"junction out of that court is directed to me "the Chancellor for the delivering the posses-"sion thereof accordingly." There is a decree in the Exchequer for restoring the church to the parish from whence it was taken. Mr. Butler concluded with this observation, that the case of St. Andrew's church was clear and decisive evidence, that, however high Lord Strafford's notions of prerogative were, however adverſe he ever was to the rights of the people, he never dreamed of an inviolability from action and the barons of that day gave an example, in the following of which, the barons of the preſent day would diſplay that independence and firmneſs which ought ever to attend the deciſion, of courts of juſtice.

Mr. Emmet, on the ſame ſide with Mr. Butler, began by commenting on the nature of this application. It was made by the Attorney General, avowing himſelf not to be Counſel for Lord Weſtmoreland; no cauſe being in Court on which to ground this application; before appearance, and unſupported by any affidavit. It was not, he ſaid, a motion, and it would not be called a motion, if the counſel on the other ſide could call it by any other name. He would however tell the court what it was, it was a *meſſage* from a great man deſiring the court to ſtop the proceſs of the law againſt him; and he would ſay, on the authority of 2 Inſt. 56. that it is exactly that againſt which the "*nulli negabimus juſtitiam*" of Magna Charta was enacted. The ground of the application, as ſtated by the Attorney General on a former occaſion, was, that Lord Weſtmoreland would not appear, and that it would be inconvenient and even dangerous to arreſt him in the midſt of his guards. If by law he cannot be compelled to appear, ſaid Mr. Emmet, the menace was unneceſſary—if by law he may be compelled to appear, the menace was *Indecent*. If he can be compelled to appear, he *muſt* appear, and notwithſtanding the character given of him by his own immediate advocates, I cannot believe, that while he claims to be the viceroy of this kingdom, he will ſet the example of reſiſting the laws to the ſubjects of his Sovereign. But by law he may be compelled to appear, no privilege exempts him from appearing; for no privilege exempts him from *being ſued*. It is a principle of the law, laid down 1ſt Com. Dig. 104. Title Action (C. 3.) that *every ſubject* of the King, eccleſiaſtical or temporal, man or woman, villein or free, may *be ſued*," ſo great was the protection to the ſubjects right of ſuing, that the Common law mode was preſerved even againſt the King until another was pointed out. For this Mr. Emmet cited 1. Com. Dig. 104 (C. 1.) until " the time of Edward 1. the King might have been ſued in all actions as a common perſon." The Court obſerving that there was a doubt expreſſed in that very paſſage as to the fact, Mr. Emmet ſaid he would cite them authorities in which no doubt was expreſſed and which would leave no doubt of the fact. He then cited 43. Ed. 3. 22. Thel. Dig. L. 4. C. 1. 3.—24. Ed. 3. 55. and having eſtabliſhed that poſition, proceeded to argue, that even ſuppoſing Lord Weſtmoreland to be what he claimed to be, Lord Lieutenant, his privilege is only an emanation from and cannot be greater than the King's prerogative.—But even the King can be ſued by petition, and would ſtill continue ſuable by the common law mode, if another, more adapted to the ſubtlety of the times, had not been, found out; therefore the Lord Lieutenant muſt ſtill continue ſuable by the common law mode, ſince he cannot be ſued in any other way. The Court have no right to quaſh its proceſs for any thing but irregularity, and none is alledged here. But the only foundation of the application, is, that an action will not lie againſt the Lord Lieutenant. That may be true, and yet he may be ſued. There are many men in many caſes against whom actions will not lie, and yet they may be sued and must appear. If the viceroy has such a privilege, he comes too soon.—he must plead it, In Mostyn versus Fabrigas Cowp. 172. Lord Mansfield says, if it were true that the law makes him that sacred character, he must plead it, and set forth his commission as special matter of Justification; because *prima facie* the court has Jurisdiction. Mr. Emmet then cited several authorities to shew that this was the Rule of all privileges, and observed that this attempt to avoid pleading and setting forth the Lord Lieutenant's Commission resulted from fear; for his counsel knew that if it was spread on the Record, it might be demurred to, and could be proved to be a nullity. This endeavour to determine the question in a summary way has also another object, to prevent the plaintiff from being able to appeal, or from taking advantage of a writ of error; but the very reason ought to induce the court to refuse the application. A question of novelty and importance ought to be put in the most solemn and conclusive mode of determination, and the Court ought to decline deciding in a manner summary and final on a matter in which the subject ought to have the power of appeal. He next questioned the *dictum* that no action will lie against a Governor locally during his Government. It is my Lord Mansfield's, said he, unsupported, as far as I know, by any other authority in the books, and fortunately my Lord Mansfield has given the reason of his opinion; "because upon process he would be subject to imprisonment." The guarded manner of expressing the *dictum* shews its weakness. He says *locally* no action lies; but he does not and could not say that no action would lie against him out of the place where he is governor, and yet his imprisonment in England would as much impede and embarrass his Government, as if it were at Barbadoes. But it is not necessary that he should be subject to imprisonment in order that an action should lie. They are every day brought against peers and persons whose bodies are privileged from arrest. If the right of the subject to have remedy for injury must be restricted by circumstances of policy, it ought only to be restricted as far as that policy renders it indispensible. The principles of the common law and the right of the subject ought not to be sacrificed even to the attainment of that great object, the security of a Viceroy's person, if it can be attained in any other way. The consequence therefore, is, that the court must so mould its process as to attain the redress of the subject without violating that privilege. This can be done by making the next process, after this subpoena, distress and not attachment, and be by letting the plaintiff proceed at his peril to a parliamentary appearance. Mr. Emmet then cited by way of analogy to his last position a case from *Raymond* 152, in which it was determined that an officer of the King's household, whose person was consequently free from arrests, might be sued, so as that the King might not be deprived of his service, and so might be outlawed. He then observed that the inconveniencies of the opposite doctrine would be most monstrous and shew it cannot be law. Mr. Butler had very forceably asked, would it be a good replication to the plea of the statute of limitations, that the Defendant was Chief Governor? He would also ask, would it be good evidence on a question of twenty years possession in ejectment, that the Defendant was Lord Lieutenant, and that therefore no action could be brought against him? Were the court prepared to ſay that a Viceroy might contract any debts, might break any contracts, might do any wrong, might commit any crimes of impunity? Were they prepared to ſay, that the King by continuing any man to be a Governor during life, might give him, not only a pardon for all crimes, but an indemnity from all civil engagements. The King himſelf has no ſuch indemnity. Were the court prepared to ſay, that no action will lie againſt him as executor or truſtee? If they are, they muſt alſo ſay, that he cannot be an executor or truſtee. The law ſays almoſt as much of the King, it ſays he ſhall not be a truſtee, and that if he be appointed executor, he ſhall delegate others againſt whom actions ſhall be brought: thus preſerving the ſubjects right to remedy. The Lord Lieutenant certainly can be a truſtee, and be ſued as ſuch; for he is one in many inſtances, and actions are brought againſt him as ſuch every day. Here Mr. Baron Power intimated that the Court knew the cauſe of action, for the Attorney General had told it to them; upon which Mr. Emmet replied, that neither the court nor the Attorney General could poſſibly know, nor had a right to know the cauſe of action, that no one but Mr. Tandy, his counſel, and his attorney could know the cauſe of action, and that the court if they decide againſt the plaintiff, muſt ſay, that no action whatſoever will lie againſt the Lord Lieutenant. But, continued Mr. Emmet, if the Governor be entitled to ſuch a privilege as is contended for, he muſt be a *legal* Governor and *legally* appointed, in as much as the privilege is a *legal* one. The Court may know that he is *de facto* Governor, and that may be ſufficient to warrant and induce them to pay him every obeiſance and attention, or perhaps to ſanction any ministerial act which he must do, but he can never have a legal right to a legal privilege in a Court of Law, unless he had a legal right to his office; but he has not a legal right to his office, for he is appointed under the Great Seal of England. It was but lately that some of the ablest lawyers, on the Bench, and at the Bar, were of opinion that the Great Seal of England could not appoint a *Regent* for this Kingdom. Is the court prepared to controvert this doctrine, by asserting the equivalent of its opposite to be true? It is prepared to say, that the Great Seal of England can appoint a Regent, for it can appoint a a Viceroy, whose name and whose functions differ but little from those of a Regent. The Attorney General deprecated on a former day the the supposition that this country has been for six hundred years without a legal Viceroy. To that, said Mr. Emmit, I answer with the sincere wish, that this country may not continue to be, as it has been for the last six hundred years; its independence was ascertained in 1782, and if there was any abuse crept in before, it ought to have ceased then. For the last ten years, I boldly say, there has been no legal Viceroy in Ireland; and the counsel for Lord Westmoreland will not only not venture to contradict me, but they will not even dare to let his patent get into a train of legal investigation. Mr. Emmet concluded, that this was an application which Lord Westmoreland had no right to make, and which the court had no right to grant.

Mr. Mc Nally, on the part of the plaintiff, wished that the counsel on the part of Lord Westmoreland should then be heard, and that he would reply. But the Court having declared that they did not require to hear counsel on behalf of Lord Westmoreland,—Mr. Mc Nally declined to speak, alledging that he could add nothing new to what had already been advanced by Mr. Butler and Mr. Emmet though he was ready to reply to the counsel on the other side.

Mr. George Joseph Brown followed Mr. M[c] Nally in saying that every thing that could have been said, having been already laid before the Court by Mr. Butler and Mr. Emmet, he would not trouble them with any observation of his—his industry had supplied him with only one Case, the Case of St. Andrew's Church and he had communicated it to Mr. Butler, who has already submitted it to the Court.

Lord Chief Baron. I wish that the counsel on behalf of Lord Westmoreland would apply themselves to one point, viz. " in what capacity is Lord Westmoreland sued" I am clearly of opinion that he is not liable to be sued for any act of state, but how does it appear that he is here sued for such act—he has two capacities, a natural and a politic capacity—the action may be against him in his natural capacity, and then the question would admit of more difficulty, tho' even then, I incline strongly to think that he is not liable to be sued, however, could it be made appear that he is sued in his politic capacity, the cause would be eased of every doubt.—I have two capacities—I am Barry Yelverton and I am chief Baron; as Barry Yelverton, I am satisfied that he is sued for an act of state, but my satisfaction as Chief Baron is not equally certain.

Mr. Prime Serjeant and Mr Soliciter General thereupon strongly insisted, that, from the argument of the plaintiffs Council, it clearly appeared that the action was brought against the Earl of Westmoreland in his public capacity and that such, was the evident tendency of the most part of what they advanced. They further insisted, that the cause of action would appear from the letter of Attorney from the plaintiff to Mr. Dowling. They also contended, that the Counsel for the Plaintiff not having denied the allegation of the Attorney General, that the action was brought against Lord Westmoreland for an act of state, joined to the refusal of Mr. Dowling the Plaintiff's Attorney to disclose the cause of action, was sufficient to ground a judicial knowledge or presumption that the action was brought against Lord Westmoreland for an act of state.

Mr. Attorney General. If the plaintiff's Counsel will declare that the action is brought against Lord Westmoreland in his natural capacity and not for an act of state, I will immediately enter appearance for his Lordship.

Lord Chief Baron. Mr. Butler, I address you as a man of candour, and desire that you will inform me of the cause of action.

Mr. Butler. I cannot comply with your Lordship's desire, but must be excused from disclosing the cause of action.

Lord Chief Baron. Then I am now satisfied that the action is brought for an act of state.

Mr. Emmet. I trust that your Lordship will not ground an admission of a fact on the refusal of Counsel to disclose it, when the Counsel is privileged in such his refusal. I trust also that nothing will be presumed from the hypothetical arguments of Counsel I cannot inform the court of the cause of action not having been instructed in respect to it.

Lord Chief Baron. I will deliver my opinion on Wednesday next.

Mr. Baron Power said that he was prepared to give his Opinion then, and that he would be sorry that the audience should go away without hearing an answer to the very extraordinary arguments they juſt heard; he ſaid that thoſe arguments were unfounded, and not warranted by Law or conſtitution, He then entered into a long and elaborate argument in favor of the conſtitution principally extracted from the firſt volume of Blackſtone's Commentaries—He ſaid that he would not give any opinion whether a Lord Lieutenant is ſuable in his natural capacity or not, it was unneceſſary, as the queſtion does not ariſe; if ſuch queſtion ever ſhould ariſe, he would feel little difficulty in forming an opinion.—He ſaid that he had judicial knowledge that the preſent action was brought againſt the Lord Lieutenant for an act of ſtate, for every matter is taken for granted when it is aſſerted on one ſide and not denied on the other, that the Attorney General had aſſerted that the action was brought for an act of ſtate, and the other ſide not having denied the aſſertion, it ſhall be conſidered as true, the action is therefore brought againſt the Lord Lieutenant for an act of State, and he declared himſelf to be clearly of opinion that for an act of State, no action could be brought againſt the Lord Lieutenant.

Mr. Emmet. Begged leave to aſſure the Court, that he was not ignorant of the principles laid down by the learned Judge; for he had read the firſt Volume of Blackſtone's Commentaries.—But he had not noticed them, becauſe he did not conceive them to apply to the preſent caſe.

Court. Let the motion ſtand over until Wedneſday next.

Wednesday, Nov. 28th.

The following LETTER of ATTORNEY was read.

Copy of a Warrant of Attorney, from James Napper Tandy, Esq. to Mathew Dowling, Attorney, to commence and prosecute Suits. Dated, April 26th, 1792.

WHEREAS, *James Napper Tandy, of Bride-street, in the City of Dublin, Esq. was arrested on the 22d day of February last, by one of the messengers attending the House of Commons, and was also arrested on the 18th day of April, inst. by one other of the said messengers which arrests were alledged to have been made under, and by the virtue of a warrant, signed by the Right Hon. John Foster, Speaker of said House. And whereas, a Proclamation has several times of late been published in the Dublin Gazette, reciting the said arrest of the 22d of February, and that said James Napper Tandy having made escape therefrom, had been guilty of a gross violation of the privileges of the said house. Also reciting and address from the House of Commons, to issue a Proclamation for apprehending said James Napper Tandy, and which Proclamation required and commanded all persons, whatsoever, to apprehend the said James Napper Tandy, and carry him before some of the Justices of the Peace, or Chief Magistrates of the county, town, or place where he should be apprehended, who are thereby respectively required to secure the said James Napper Tandy, so apprehended, and thereof to give speedy notice to the Right Hon. the Speaker of the House of Commons, the Serjeant at Arms attending the said house, and to the Clerk of the Council, to the end he may be forthcoming to be dealt withal and pre-*

ceeded against according to law. And that for the prevention of the escape of the said James Napper Tandy, into parts beyond the seas, said proclamation did require and command all officers of the customs, and other officers and subjects of and in the respective ports, and maritime towns, and places within the kingdom of Ireland, that they and every of them in their respective places and stations, within the said kingdom, should be careful and diligent in the examination of all persons that should pass or endeavour to pass beyond the seas, and that if they should discover the said James Napper Tandy, then to cause him to be apprehended and secured, and to give notice thereof as aforesaid. And the said Proclamation did also strictly charge and command all persons as they would answer the contrary at their perils, that they should not any way conceal, but should discover the said James Napper Tandy, to the end he might be secured. And for the encouragement of all persons to be diligent and careful in endeavouring to discover and apprehend the said James Napper Tandy, said Proclamation did further declare, that whosoever should discover and apprehend him, the said James Napper Tandy, and should bring him before some Justice of the Peace, or Chief Magistrate, as aforesaid, should have and receive as a reward for the discovering, apprehending, and bringing him the said James Napper Tandy, before such Justice of the Peace, or Chief Magistrate, as aforesaid, the sum of fifty pounds. And whereas the said James Napper Tandy was arrested by a man of the name of John Knight, and kept in custody for half an hour, and it was alledged by said Knight that such arrest was made by him in obedience to and by virtue or under colour of said Proclamation.——Now, know all men by these presents, that I, the said James Napper Tandy, do hereby constitute, and appoint, *direct, authorize and impower Mathew Dowling, of Great Longford street, in the city of Dublin, gent. one of the Attorney's of his Majesty's Courts of Exchequer, King's Bench, and Common Pleas, in Ireland, to commence, institute, carry on and prosecute one or more action or actions at my suit and in my name against such members of the Privy Council as signed the said Proclamation, also against the Printers or Publishers of the Newspaper called the Dublin Gazette, and against the said John Knight, or to prosecute the said Knight, and also against the Right Hon. John Foster, Speaker of the House of Commons, the Serjeant at Arms, and Messengers attending the said House, the Sheriffs of the county of the city of Dublin, the Gaoler of the New Prison, and all and every person and persons who acted in any manner under the said Warrant or Proclamation. And for these purposes to take all such steps and proceedings in any of the law or other courts as he may be advised, or deem necessary or expedient. Hereby, ratifying, allowing, and confirming all, and whatsoever my said Attorney shall do, or cause or direct to be done in the premises. In witness whereof, I have hereunto set my Hand and Seal, this 26th day of April in the Year of our Lord, 1792.*

Signed, Sealed and Delivered in the presence of us, } *J. N. TANDY, Seal.*
THOMAS DOWLING
JAS. NEWENHAM CURTIS.

Lord Chief Baron. I am now ready to own that I am glad I postponed giving my opinion to this time, because a document has been read which throws new light upon the subject, and which shews the action to be commenced against Lord *Westmoreland* for an act done in his politic capacity. The question therefore is not a general one, " whether a Lord Lieutenant in his government may be sued for an act of power,"—but, " whether he may be sued for an act of *State*," I did very early declare, that no man could maintain an action against a Lord Lieutenant for an act of State during his government. The acts of State done by a Lord Lieutenant, like those of the King, are all countersigned by responsible ministers, and if he be advised to do any thing unconstitutional by them, they are responsible for it—but I do not found this opinion upon any distinction betweeen the natural and politic capacity in the person of the Lord Lieutenant. There is not any distinction of that kind that does not apply equally to the King: he performs in his natural capacity all the functions of nature: he eats, drinks, and sleeps:—and any other act done by him, whether public or private, is done by him as a corporation sole, and therefore it is, he cannot depart from any matter of state but by matter of record, and this does not extend less in the case of a Lord Lieutenant, I found my opinion upon the broadest grounds: not upon the law of any particular state, but upon the law of nature and nations, It is a question in which not Ireland or Great Britain only are concerned, but every orderly government.—I found it upon this, that so long as he is Governor, so long as he is the executive power, he cannot be called upon. Antiently he enjoyed many more privileges than he does now almost every prerogative which the Crown Enjoys at this day, he once had; it appears from history he declared peace and war and gave the Royal assent, *rege inconsulto*.—Now, it is not given, but in the name of the King.—There is an entry in the Journals, *Le Seigneur Depute le veut*. But now by a wholesome law these powers are reſtrained. But ſtill he cannot be ſued. In every country there is ſome authority lodged ſomewhere: this power is divided into the legiſlative, the executive and the Judicial, and it is from the different combinations of thoſe three different powers that ariſes all the difference of the Governments exiſting in the world.—But where there is an executive power particularly, it is neceſſary to the end of Government it ſhould be ſacred and inviolable; for the moment the liberty of the perſon of the executive power is reſtrained, the moment the free agency is taken away, that inſtant the Government falls, there is an end of all Government, the moment the executive power is violated. I have ſaid, this is not a queſtion merely of the municipal Law of Ireland or England, but of the Law of Nations, and to ſhew that it is, look into *Puffendorf de Officio hominis & civis* treating not of the law of this ſtate or that, but of the law of Nations.—He ſays, " If the ſubject be aggrieved by a ſovereign he cannot maintain an action, or oblige him to redreſs, he may perſuade him if he can"—But look at higher authority, that of the celebrated *Lock in his Eſſay on Government*: he lays down the ſame poſition, and he founds it, not upon any diſtinction between the natural and politic capacity, but upon this broad bottom, that it is better a private miſchief ſhould enſue to an Individual, than the peace and ſecurity of Government ſhould be violated by any Attack upon the Magiſtrate Executing the power of ſtate. —He puts the caſe of a heady Prince coming to the Throne and doing private acts of miſchief, but altho' theſe miſchief, may exiſt, they happen ſo rarely, and travel thro' ſo ſmall an extent, it is better to put up with them"—This, it is obſerved, is carried ſo far in the caſe of a King, that even for a matter of private concern, he cannot be sued otherwise than by petition, bringing it to the case in *Puffendorf*, he may persuade if he can, but he cannot compel him; and therefore it is upon that ground, that the King is suable by petition or *monstrans de droit*, and this whether the matter be of a public or private nature, and if I were called upon for an opinion whether the Lord Lieutenant can be sued for an act of a private nature; I would say he cannot perhaps he may be sued in *auter droit*; but with respect to himself he cannot. If process could issue against him his person might be imprisoned, he might be seized under colour of a suit, even when going to Exercise one of the Royal functions committed to his charge; when going to meet the Parliament of the Country. If this doctrine could be maintained, he might have been arrested when going to give the Royal assent to that act which established our right of being an ancient independant Kingdom.—But it is said great mischiefs will follow; limitations will run; a Lord Lieutenant may be continued for life; he may do wrong, and the subject be without redress.—To that I answer, it is indecent to put any such case, and it might as well be put in the case of a King; he may do wrong, commit murder, assassination, injury of every kind, and the subject is equally without redress. But the law will not admit any such notion and it is highly indecent for us to suppose it. But I am happily relieved from the necessity of giving any opinion upon the " point whether he may be sued for any act done by him in a private capacity," when it appears now, by unquestionable evidence under the hand and seal of the plaintiff, he avows he sues him for an act done by him as Lord Lieutenant,—I am satisfied he cannot be sued in that capacity, and therefore the motion muſt be granted, namely, the proceſs ought to be quaſhed as having iſſued improvidently.—With regard to what has been ſaid about the letter miſſive, it is true, I was applied to for it, but the reaſon which weighed with me for refuſing it, was, that if I ſigned it, I would give my ſanction to the proceſs; whereas I wiſhed it ſhould ſtand upon its own ſtrength or weakneſs. A paſſage was cited from Strafford's letters.—I looked into the book and I find it was truly cited; but it cannot be received as law now.—One of the deputies had been ſerved with an injunction commanding him to give poſſeſſion of Patrick's church which had been uſed as a ſtable. —Put the caſe that the Chancellor forming a part of the executive Government had refuſed to obey—his perſon might be taken and what would become of the executive power, the Government would be ſuſpended; it is better, I ſay, that a private injury ſhould be ſuſtained by an individual, than that there ſhould be no Government in the country; and how ready people are to contend that there is no Government in the country is evident, as it was argued by the gentlemen, who, to do them juſtice, ſpoke ably, that we were at this inſtant actually without any legal Government; for they did aſſert and argue we had no legal Lord Lieutenant in the country. —It is unneceſſary to argue that we have *de ſtricto jure*—while in the executive power of Government he is Governor *pro hac vice*.

N. B. In the caſe of Lord Donegal againſt Hamilton, in giving his opinion the ſame day, the Lord Chief Baron ſaid, I am unwilling to give my opinion whether the King has a right to grant any thing in this kingdom under any ſeal but the great ſeal of this his kingdom of Ireland: but I confeſs I am inclined to think at preſent that he cannot."

Mr. Baron Hamilton. I do not wiſh to reſort to any doctrine of our court, or law of this country to ſupport my opinion; I found myſelf upon principles that muſt belong to every Government in the world—The queſtion is, ſhall we ſuffer a proceſs to iſſue, where the Executive power of this Government may be put into reſtraint, I may ſay into priſon.—I beg to know, can ſuch a proceeding as that be found in the hiſtory of mankind?—In any Government, however free, the moſt democratical that ever exiſted, even in France, notwithſtanding all their confuſion, they hold the Executive power inviolable. Can any Government exiſt, if there be not an Executive authority to carry the laws into execution.—What will avail all your laws if it be in the power of an individual to iſſue out proceſs and confine the executive authority. It is very well known that the acts of a Governor relate to every one; what a monſtrous doctrine it would be, that every one of the individuals who feel themſelves aggrieved or affected by the proceedings of a Governor, ſhould have a power each to bring an action; the Law of the country would become uſeleſs; no government could ſubſiſt if that procedure prevailed.—The counſel for the plaintiff could not avow that the Governor could be ſued in his public capacity, becauſe they refuſed to declare in what right he was ſued.

Mr. Butler humbly conceived that the Lord Chief Baron was miſtaken in a matter of fact, in conceiving that the warrant of attorney, which had been read, had any relation to this cauſe; it gives no authority to Mr. Dowling to ſue the Earl of Weſtmoreland either in his politic or natural capacity, and is not therefore any evidence, under hand and ſeal of the plaintiff; of this action being brought againſt Lord Weſtmoreland as Lord Lieutenant, for an act of ſtate or otherwiſe.

Lord Chief Baron. If you had done me the honour to attend to me, you would perceive my reaſon for noticing the letter of attorney, which though it does not authorize an action againſt Lord Weſtmoreland, yet in a great meaſure explains and gives a complexion to the whole tranſaction, upon the whole I am ſatisfied that this action is inſtituted againſt the Lord Lieutenant in his politic capacity.

Court, Let the ſubpœna be quaſhed.

James N. Tandy, Eſq. againſt The Right Hon. Arthur Wolf. } THE declaration in this caſe was filed on the 15th day of November, 1792. It is for cauſing to be printed and publiſhed an unlawful and libellous publication and conſiſts of four counts.—firſt, an unlawful publication in the words and figures—ſecond an unlawful publication to the tenor.—third, a libellous publication in the words and figures, and fourth a libellous publication to the tenor.—The publication complained of by the declaration was a proclamation purporting to be iſſued by the Lord Lieutenant and council of Ireland commanding the arreſt of the plaintiff and offering a reward for the ſame, in the declaration the proclamation is ſet forth in manner following—" By the Lord Lieutenant" (meaning the Right Hon. John Fane Earl of Weſtmoreland of the kingdom of Great Britain commonly called but not of right the Lieutenant General and General Governor) " and council", (meaning the assembly of persons commonly called but not of right the Right Hon. the privy counsel) of Ireland " A proclamation Westmoreland" meaning the aforesaid Right Honourable John Fane Earl of Westmoreland of the kingdom of Great Britain) " Whereas" &c. &c.

The ground for using these expressions was, that the Earl of Westmoreland received his appointment as Lord Lieutenant of Ireland under the Great Seal of Great Britain, and that consequently he was not legally Lord Lieutenant of Ireland, or such a person as could receive the oath of a privy counsellor.

On Wednesday the 28th of November 1792 Mr. Franklyn, on behalf of the defendant, moved that the declaration filed in this cause might be taken off the file, or that such parts thereof as alledged " that the present chief Governor of " this kingdom is not so of right, and that the " present privy counsel of this kingdom is not of " right, the privy counsel thereof" might be expunged; and in case the court should refuse to take the declaration off the file, that the defendant might have time to plead until the next Term.

Baron Power. This is a motion of course—refer it to a Baron.

Lord Chief Baron, No.—I will not refer it—I will expunge the scandalous parts *instanter*. Let the declaration be read.

The Declaration was hereupon read.

Mr. Baron Power. I concur with the Chief Baron.—I will expunge the scandal instantly—those passages are prolix, impertinent and scandalous—I do not stop here; those who signed the declaration should be punished.

Lord Chief Baron. Who signed the declaration?

Mr. Kemmis, the agent for the defendant, read the names "Simon Butler and Thomas Addis Emmet." as thoſe ſigned to the declaration.

Lord Chief Baron. Who is attorney for the plaintiff?

He was anſwered that the attorney was Matthew Dowling.

Mr. Butler. It was not my intention to trouble the court this day.—After what I heard from the court on Monday—after what I have heard this day from the bench—after what has paſſed this day in the court of common pleas, where though I could not offer my ſentiments on behalf of my client, on account of the motion having been made on the part of his Majeſty, yet where I had the the ſatisfaction of hearing every thing ſaid and urged on behalf of the plaintiff that could be ſaid or urged—I ſay, my lord, that after the very decided opinion of the court, I ſhould merely have entered my proteſt to the order ſought for by the defendant—but as a threat has been thrown out from the bench againſt thoſe who have ſigned the declaration, it becomes my duty to enter at large into the motion, and ſhew to the ſatisfaction of every honeſt and unprejudiced mind, that the parts ſought to be expunged from the declaration are not prolix ſcandalous or impertinent, but relevant and neceſſary to the plaintiff's caſe.

Lord Chief Baron. What threat has been thrown out! I know of none.

Baron Power. You intirely miſunderſtand the court—I did not allude to the gentlemen of the bar who ſigned the declaration—I alluded to the Attorney whoſe name appeared to the declaration.

Mr. Butler. I am happy to hear that the court did not allude to or mean to cenſure the gentlemen of the bar who ſigned the declaration—but as the court is pleaſed to ſay that they alluded to the attorney, Mr. Dowling, who ſigned the declaration as attorney for the plaintiff. I requeſt to be heard a few words. Mr. Dowling is merely agent—he acts by the direction and is under the controul of counſel—the warrant of attorney which the court has before them, directs that he ſhould act under the direction and be ſubject to the controul of counſel——having informed your lordſhips what the duty of Mr. Dowling is, I will now inform you, that he has performed it—and in no reſpect exceeded it—every act done by him in this cauſe has been by the direction and from the advice and under the controul of counſel,—He has not in any reſpect acted from himſelf or independant of the advice and even direction of counſel——He is not reſponſible, he has only performed his duty—If there has been any impropriety, the counſel are to be blamed—If any cenſure is to fall, let it fall upon the counſel; and if any puniſhment is to be inflicted, let it be received by the counſel—I make this declaration publicly as one of the counſel, and if I had not, I would be aſhamed ever to raiſe my voice again in this or any other court.

Mr. Butler was followed by Mr. Emmet, who, as one of the counſel declared his reſponſibility, and that Mr. Dowling, throughout the buſineſs, acted merely as attorney and under the expreſs direction of counſel.

Lord Chief Baron. I am not decided in my mind as to the courſe which ought to be taken by the Court on this occaſion—we will conſider of it, and do what ſhall appear to be proper.

Mr. Butler. It is then my duty to enter at large into the cauſe and ſhew to the court, that the words in queſtion are not prolix, ſcandalous, or impertinent, but that on the contrary they are relevant to and very material for the plaintiff's caſe.

Lord Chief Baron.—You are certainly at liberty to ſatisfy the court, if you can, as to the relevancy of the words; but in ſo doing, I muſt inform you that the court will not ſuffer you to queſtion the legality of the Lord Lieutenant's patent—that point ſhall not again be argued in this Court.

Mr. Butler. They ſeek to expunge the words, "commonly called but not of right"—Before I ſhew the relevancy, I will ſhew the truth of the words—I will ſhew that the Earl of Weſtmoreland is not of right the Lord Lieutenant of Ireland, and that the privy Council are not of right the privy Council of Ireland.

Lord Chief Baron. I will not ſuffer that matter to be argued; I have already told you ſo——I repeat it—From the ferment of the Public mind, I do not know whether I ſhall ſit another year upon this Bench; but were this the laſt time of my ſitting here, I would reſiſt every attempt to ſhew that there is no legal executive power in the country.

Baron Hamilton. This may poſſibly be the laſt year of my life, but were it the laſt moment of my life, I would not ſuffer any man to argue that there is no legal executive power in the country.

Mr. Butler. I did hope that I ſhould have been permitted to argue the caſe of my client in ſuch manner as to me ſeemed moſt adviſeable—I recollect the conduct of the firſt advocate of England, when directed by the majority of the Houſe of Commons to confine his argument on behalf of his client to certain points; Mr. Erſkine declared, that in the argument of his client's caſe, he would not be dictated to by any power, and that unleſs he was permitted to argue the caſe of his clients in ſuch manner as he thought moſt for the benefit of his clients, he would not make any argument.—I will follow ſo great an example, and declare to this court and to the Nation that, as I am not permitted to argue the cauſe of my client in ſuch manner as I think moſt for his benefit, I will ſit down.

Lord Chief Baron. I am far from dictating to any gentleman the manner of laying his client's caſe before the court—it is not my nature—and it never was my practice but I muſt again declare, that I will not ſuffer any perſon to argue that there is no legal Chief Governor in this country.

Court.—Let the words be expunged and let the defendant have time to plead until the firſt day of next term.

James N. Tandy, Eſq. againſt Timothy Dyton and St. Geo. O'Kelly, Eſqrs.

THIS is an action for printing and publiſhing and cauſing to be printed and publiſhed an unlawful and libelous publication, and contains four counts ſimilar to thoſe in the laſt mentioned action.

Mr. Frankland on behalf of the defendants moved the court for liberty to withdraw the plea filed by the defendants, and that the declaration might be taken off the file, or that thoſe parts thereof wherein it is alledged that the preſent Chief Governor of this kingdom is not ſo of right and that the preſent privy council of this kingdom is not of right the privy council thereof might be expunged.

Counſel on behalf of Mr. Tandy were ſilent.

Court.—Let the defendants have liberty to withdraw the plea, and let the words be expunged, and let the defendants have time to plead to the first day of next term.

James N. Tandy Esq. against The Right Hon. John Foster.	THIS is an action for false imprisonment on the 22d. of February and 5th of May 1792.

Mr. Frankland, on behalf of the defendant, moved the court for time to plead until the next term.

Mr. Frankland, said, that no tryal would be thereby lost, as the defendant would justify under an order of the House of Commons.

Counsel for the plaintiff were silent.

Court. Let defendant have time to plead until first day of next term.

Wednesday 28th November, 1792.

COMMON PLEAS.

James N. Tandy Esq. Plaintiff
The Right Hon. John Lord Baron Fitzgibbon Defendant:

THIS is an action for causing to be printed and published an unlawful and libellous publication, and contains four Counts similar to those contained in the declaration against Mr. Wolfe.

Mr. Attorney General, on behalf of his *Majesty*, moved that the writ of summons might be superseded, and that the Declaration might be taken off the file, or that such parts thereof as alledge that the present Chief Governor of this Kingdom is not so of right, and that the present privy Council of this Kingdom is not of right the privy Council thereof, might be exgunged.

Mr. Attorney General said, it was not only Competent to him, as Attorney General, to inform the Court of any matter, but, in particular Cases, it was Competent to any man to give such information to the Judges, as *amicus Curiæ*. He had a right to do so, as *amicus Curiæ*, when any Indecency, Immorality or matter injurious to the state, appeared upon the Record of the Court, in order that such matter should be expunged. The declaration or Bill which had been put upon the file of the Court by the plaintiff against the defendant, and the writ of summons which issued thereupon, he considered seditious in tendency, scandalous to the state, and insulting to the Court. 'Tis said that the Lord Lieutenant of Ireland was not Lord Lieutenant of right, that the privy Council of Ireland is not privy Council of right. This is not less than alledging that there was no Government in the Country. He trusted that the Court would immediately, peremptorily and unequivocally decide upon the motion he had made, that the dangerous and absurd idea, of the Country being without a Government, might not for a moment go abroad to deceive and to mislead the people. If the suggestion was true, the Court had no jurisdiction, the Judges had no authority to act under. The Council who drew the Bill and advised the measure, were not, he presumed, apprized how Lord Lieutenants were appointed. They were, and had been for six hundred years past, appointed by the King's will, made known under the great seal of England annexed to Letters patent; when he arrives in this country, the sword of state is delivered into his hands, in the presence of the Council, by those who preceded him in office, and he takes the usual Oaths—This is the only legal mode of appointing a Lord Lieutenant——

Mr. Justice Hellen, coincide with the Attorney General that the Court should immediately decide upon the question, The suggestion that the Earl of Westmoreland was not Lord Lieutenant of Ireland of right, and the Privy Council Privy Council of right, he considered a position fraught with the most dangerous Consequences.

The Chief Justice, inquired if any Counsel attended on the part of the plaintiff.

Mr. Mc. Nally answered, that he and Mr. Emmet were of Counsel for the plaintiff Mr. Tandy; that he was not unprepared as to the question hereafter to come before the Court, if the defendant thought proper to justify by plea or by Evidence, for he had considered the question, and prepared himself with sedulous industry; but he thought it would be imprudent in him at this early ſtage of the proceedings againſt the Defendant to communicate the principles and grounds upon which he propoſed hereafter to contend, that the appointment of the Earl of Weſtmoreland to the Office of Lord Lieutenant was not legal, but, on the contrary, inconſiſtent with the Conſtitution of this Country.

He obſerved that Attorney General had come forward as an *amicus curiæ*—this was the firſt time he had ever ſeen an *amicus curiæ* come forward to make a motion with a Brief in his hand, and that Brief marked with a fee—an *amicus curiæ* was authorized to inform the Court of matter of Law if the Court was in Error, but until this day he had never heard an *amicus curiæ* attempt to argue as council for a party upon motion—Here—

Mr. Juſtice Hellen interrupted Mr. Mc. Nally who, his Lordſhip ſaid, muſt have miſunderſtood the Attorney General; for the Attorney General had not ſtated that he had appeared as an *amicus curiæ* but that an *amicus curiæ* might with propriety give the ſame Information to the Court as he was going to give in his character of Attorney General.

Mr. Mc. Nally aſſured the Court that he had not the ſlighteſt intention to miſtate what had fallen from his Majeſty's leading Counſel; a Gentleman for whoſe learning and abilities he had the higheſt reſpect; but he was led into the miſtake by a very extraordinary ſignature which appeared at the bottom of the Notice ſerved upon his Client. The whole Caſe before the Court was extraordinary and novel, but perhaps the ſignature to the Notice was the moſt extraordinary and novel that ever appeared in Court. The Notice was ſigned " Thomas Kemmis, Attorney to his Majeſty," now if Thomas Kemmis was Attorney to his Majeſty, in what ſituation was the Right Hon. Arthur Wolfe? were there two Attorney Generals—Attorney General Wolfe and Attorney General Kemmis? or did Mr. Attorney General Wolfe ſlide out of his place *pro tempore*, for the purpoſe of letting Mr. Thomas Kemmis ſlip in *pro tempore*, and act as Attorney General in the actions pending againſt the Privy Counſellors who cauſed the advertiſement in queſtion to be publiſhed? If that was the Caſe, he was warranted in ſuppoſing that the Right Hon. Arthur Wolfe was acting ſolely in the ſituation of an *amicus curiæ*,——

Mr. Mc Nally then argued, that the notice was bad—It was bad as being too general. It called upon the Court to expunge certain words, but it did not ſtate any Cauſe for expunging thoſe words—it did not ſtate that thoſe words were ſuperfluous, impertinent or ſcandalous? whereas; it ſhould have ſpecially ſtated at leaſt one of thoſe cauſes whether the words complained of deſerved the epithets applied to them, he truſted the Court would not now determine, but grant a conditional order that the plaintiff's Counſel might ſhew Cauſe why they ſhould not be expunged.

Mr. Solicitor General and Mr. Prime Serjeant ſaid a few words each to the queſtion, in which they followed.

Mr. Attorney General, in ſtigmatizing the words excepted to, as being in their tendency ſeditious and ſcandalous. They applied to the court that the Sheriff ſhould inſtantly return the writ of ſummons; which being, together with the declaration or bill, brought into court, and the words complained of read by the officer, the Attorney General, having made a few further obſervations on the pernicious effects of the words " but not of right," called on the court inſtantly to ſuperſede the writ and expunge the words from the declaration, and not merely grant a conditional order.

The Court, thereupon, called on Mr. Tandy's counſel to ſhew cauſe *inſtanter* why the writ of ſummons ſhould not be ſuperſeded, and the words " but not of right" expunged from the declaration or bill.

Mr. Emmet, hoped the court would only grant a conditional order, when he aſſured them, that he himſelf was then exceedingly indiſpoſed, and utterly unable to do his client juſtice, and when he further informed them, that, in conſequence of the motion being made on behalf of his Majeſty, Mr. Tandy was deprived of the benefit of Mr. Butler's aſſiſtance, who as king's counſel, conceived himſelf precluded from opening his mouth, until he could obtain a licence. The court expreſſing their reſolution to determine the queſtion without further delay, *Mr. Emmet* proceeded.

He acknowledged that he had ſigned the declaration or bill on which the writ of ſummons was grounded. This he thought it neceſſary to ſay in conſequence of the many charges of ſcandal and ſedition that had been thrown out againſt that declaration or bill. If the allegation which denied the authority of the Lord Lieutenant was ſeditious, who was anſwerable for that ſedition, but thoſe who dragged it from out of the peaceful obſcurity of a record of the court and forced it into public attention? If any of the evil conſequences mentioned by the Attorney General were likely to enſue from ſuch a diſcuſſion they muſt be imputed—not to the plaintiff's counſel who had inſerted the allegation in law pleadings, which few or none would ever ſee, and where it was material to their clients action,—But to the officious officers of the crown, who had given publicity to the assertion, they were unable to refute; who had selected it for argument in a crowded court; and by premature motions rendered the discussion necessary. It would have been wiser in them silently to correct the error in the Viceroy's appointment; than to shew a pertinacious attachment to an abuse, after the principle of English Supremacy, from which the abuse has grown, had been abandoned. Or if there be no such error, why do they not justify and bring the question forward on a solemn argument on the pleadings rather than endeavour to crush it by the summary mode of motion. Having pursued these observations to some length, he insisted on it as a rule of law, that the court would never expunge any matter from a declaration or bill, however scandalous or seditious it might be, if it was necessary to the plaintiff's cause of action, or if it went in aggravation of damages—apply that rule here—Suppose the proclamation complained of to be in its nature and tendency such as a legal Chief Governor and privy council would have been well warranted in issuing, yet surely it would in itself be sufficient to give the plaintiff a right of Action, if it were issued by persons having no authority so to do, and who had *accroached* to themselves nothing less than a sovereignty which did not belong to them; and assumed the place of the executive power. If the Proclamation was in itself illegal and insufficient to resist an action, yet even there it would exceedingly increase the injury, and would go in aggravation of damages that such an illegal Proclamation was issued by such persons as he had already described.

There was another reason why the court ought not to expunge the words excepted to; they would never make any alteration in any part of a suitor's pleadings that might lay them open to a demurrer. He did not absolutely say that was the case here; but it certainly was a matter of some doubt whether if those words were expunged the defendant might not demur to the declaration or bill; and he trusted the court would not comply with the motion until they were ascertained that that could not be the case.

In arguing on this motion he had hitherto taken it for granted, that Lord Westmoreland *was not of right* the Lord Lieutenant of Ireland. It was no more than the truth.—The counsel for the crown, in order to excite the pride and prejudices of the court, had said that the plaintiff's counsel denied its jurisdiction in certain cases, in as much as certain of its processes were signed by the Lord Lieutenant. He would be exceedingly sorry that the jurisdiction of that court was necessarily connected with the mode of the Viceroys appointment—his acts with regard to that court were merely ministerial; but even if he said that the power of the court ceased for the present, in consequence of the illegal appointment of the Viceroy, he did not argue against its jurisdiction in the abstract, and he only urged an additional motive for correcting the illegality. It ought not to offend the court even if he did assert an occasional suspension of its jurisdiction in certain cases. All the courts of Westminster Hall asserted the same thing of themselves in every case at the revolution; for when it was declared that King James had abdicated, they all shut, and continued so until the vacant Throne was filled by the appointment of William.

The Attorney General had almost confessed, that the objection against Lord Westmoreland's appointment was irresistible from his mode of anſvering it. He had ſaid that the patent under the great ſeal of England was only a declaration of the King's will—that is, tacitly Confeſſing that it was not competent to do more than barely declare the King's will—but if ſuch a declaration only was ſufficient, that was done by the order to be ſworn in that every Lord Lieutenant brings over under the ſign manual; or why was he not appointed merely by delivering to him the ſword of ſtate?—the reaſon is, becauſe, to the appointment of a Governor, not only a declaration of the King's will is neceſſary, but alſo a delegation of power by a ſufficient and legal inſtrument giving him a right to exerciſe authority. But no power belonging to the independent King of Ireland can be delegated by an inſtrument that derives all its validity from the authority of the King of England. The Great Seal of England cannot conſtitute an officer to act under the authority of the King of Ireland.

The Attorney General had argued a good deal on all Lord Lieutenants having been ſo appointed for upwards of ſix hundred years. The argument is not fair;—many abuſes crept into this country for the laſt ſix hundred years, becauſe its conſtitutional connection with England was but little known or attended to. If that had not been the caſe, there would have been no neceſſity for the revolution in 1782. Since that time it might be fairly aſſerted that there has not been a legally appointed Chief Governor in Ireland.—But wherefore was this abuſe ſuffered to remain after the other abuſes aboliſhed by that revolution, or wherefore was it ſo obſtinately contended for at preſent, if it was not retained for ſome evil purpoſe? Mr. Emmet concluded by hoping the Court would not do ſo great an injuſtice to the plaintiff as to expunge from his declaration or bill that which was true and which was alſo *material* to his action.

The Chief Juſtice aſked Mr. Mc. Nally whether he intended to offer any thing further againſt the motion.

Mr. Mc. Nally ſaid he was certainly fully prepared to prove before his country, that the Great Seal of England was incompetent to appoint any legal juriſdiction or office of ſtate in Ireland; which, ſince the revolution or 1782, could not be conſidered as bound by any delegated power from the Crown of Great Britain. Whenever the authority of Ireland came to be queſtioned, whether in the Common Pleas, the King's Bench, or before parliament, he had no doubt of being able to ſhew from conſtitutional principles, illuſtrated by ſacred authorities, that Letters Patent under the Great Seal of Great Britain were inefficient and inoperative in Ireland——He had determined not to ſpeak to this queſtion till it came in a more ſolemn manner before the court by the pleading of the defendant, but as the point had been broken by the motion before the court, he would make one obſervation which he conſidered of weight—it was this. In 1782 it became a queſtion in what manner the royal aſſent ſhould be given to bills, the King of Ireland being reſident in Great Britain, and a bill was brought into the Iriſh Commons, he believed by Mr. Yelverton, now Lord Chief Baron, to adjuſt that very ſerious point. By this Bill it enacted, that all Bills, in order to receive the royal aſſent, ſhould be tranſmitted to England under the Great Seal of Ireland, and having received the royal aſſent there, be returned under the Great Seal of England into Ireland. Now, ſaid Mr. Mc. Nally, if, in the opinion of the Legiſlature of Ireland, the Great Seal of England had recognition in Ireland, why enact a Statute to give it recognition in any particular instance? This act he said might be considered as an exception, strengthening the general and great constitutional position then before the Court, that the Great Seal of England was not recognized in this independant country.

Mr. Attorney General assured the court that it was not the intention of the Chancellor to delay the trial; but that his Lordship would take defence with all possible expedition.

Lord Carleton. This writ of summons having been returned, and an attested copy of the Declaration or Bill having been produced, the proceedings are before the court, and they have judicial knowledge of the exceptionable parts.

The question is narrowed by what has fallen from the plaintiff's counsel; they deny that the Lord Lieutenant has legal authority. and the court ought not to entertain a doubt for a moment of its duty to satisfy the public that there is a legal government in the country. The manner in which the question has been discussed forces the court to this declaration, for if the arguments of counsel be just, there neither is, nor has been for ages past, a legal government in Ireland.

It is true as has been stated by one of the plaintiff's counsel, that, if scandalous matter inserted in the declaration or bill be relevant, and has a tendency to encrease damages, the court will not expunge it merely because it is scandalous matter; but that it is not the case hear.—It is not relevant to, or material for the plaintiff's case, and therefore the insertion of it was not necessary.

The court will take notice that Lord Westmoreland is legally Lord Lieutenant of Ireland.

The court of Exchequer has decided ſo, and the public good requires that we ſhould decide ſo.

We are bound to know the privy council and its powers, we are bound to know it as a privy council by right.

An objection was once made in the court of Common Pleas, in a caſe wherein Baron Power was the plaintiff, that it did not appear upon the record that he was one of the King's Judges ; but we were bound to take notice judicially, that he was one of the King's Judges : and ſo we are bound to take notice judicially, that the Earl of Weſtmoreland is Lord Lieutenant of Ireland, and that the privy council are the privy council of Ireland.

The inſertion, as I have before ſaid, was not neceſſary. If the publication complained of by the plaintiff be a libel, that will be matter for further inveſtigation. The authority from whence it iſſued muſt either be ſhewn in a plea of juſtification or in evidence upon a trial, and, if the queſtion can poſſibly be agitated, then will be the plaintiff's time to controvert it.

The writ of ſummons has been returned, and is now in court; though it bears the ſignature of the Chief Juſtice, it never undergoes, but iſſues without his inſpection.

If any evil conſequences enſue from this diſcuſſion, they muſt be imputed to the plaintiff, and thoſe concerned for him, who inſerted the exceptionable words in the pleadings, and not to the Officers of the Crown, who brought forward the motion.

The other three Juſtices coincided with the Chief, and it was.

Ordered,

That the Writ of Summons be quashed, and the words which alledge or question that John Earl of Westmoreland, is not of right Lord Lieutenant of Ireland, or that the Privy Council of Ireland, is not the Privy Council thereof, wherever they occur in the declaration or Bill, be forthwith expunged by the proper officer, the same being scandalous and impertinent.

BY THE LORD LIEUTENANT AND COUNCIL OF

IRELAND,

A PROCLAMATION

WESTMORELAND,

WHEREAS the Serjeant at Arms of the Honorable House of Commons, being called before the said House on Wednesday the Twenty-second Day of February Instant, he informed the said House that he had dispatched Three of the messengers attending said House, to execute the order for taking into his Custody James Napper Tandy, one of whom being brought to the Bar, informed the House, that he went to the Dwelling-House of James Tandy in Chancery-lane, where he arrested the said James Napper Tandy, and shewed him the Warrant, and his Authority; that the said James Napper Tandy went into a Parlour, as if for his Hat, but shut the door, and made his Escape, as he supposed through a Window.

AND whereas on the same day, it was resolved by the House of Commons, that the said James Napper Tandy having been arrested by a warrant Mr. Speaker, issued by the Order of the said House and having made his Escape from the Officer of said House who arrested him, has been guilty of of a gross Violation of the Privileges of the said House.

AND whereas an humble Address hath been presented unto us, by the Knights, Citizens and Burgesses, in Parliament assembled, that we would be graciously pleased to issue our Proclamation for apprehending the said James Napper Tandy, with a Promise of Reward for the same.

NOW we, the Lord Lieutenant and Council, have thought fit to issue this our Proclamation, hereby requiring and commanding all Persons whatsoever to discover and apprehend, or cause the said James Napper Tandy to be discovered and apprehended, and carry him before some of our Justices of the Peace, or Chief Magistrates of the County, town, or Place where he shall be apprehended, who are respectively required to secure the said James Napper Tandy so apprehended, and thereof to give speedy notice to the Right Honourable the Speaker of the House of commons, the Serjeant at Arms attending the said House, and to the Clerk of the Council, to the end he may be forthcoming to be dealt withal, and proceeded against according to Law.

AND for the Prevention of the Escape of the said James Napper Tandy into Parts beyond the Seas, we do require and command all Officers of the Customs, and other Officers and Subjects of and in the respective Ports and Maritime Towns, and Places within the Kingdom of Ireland, that they and every of them in their respective Places and Stations within the said Kingdom, be careful and diligent in the Examination of all Persons that shall pass, or endeavour to pass beyond the Seas; and if they shall discover the said James Napper Tandy, then to cause him to be apprehended and secured, and to give Notice thereof as aforesaid.

AND we do hereby ſtrictly Charge and Command all Perſons, as they will anſwer the contrary at their Perils, that they do not any ways conceal, but to diſcover him, the ſaid James Napper Tandy, to the End he may be ſecured; and for the Encouragement of all Perſons to be diligent and careful in endeavouring to diſcover and apprehend the ſaid James Napper Tandy, we do hereby further declare, that whoſoever ſhall diſcover and apprehend him, the ſaid James Napper Tandy, and ſhall bring him before ſome Juſtice of the Peace, or Chief Magiſtrate as aforeſaid, ſhall have and receive as a Reward for the diſcovering, apprehending and bringing him, the ſaid James Napper Tandy, before ſuch Juſtice of the Peace, or Chief Magiſtrate as aforeſaid, the Sum of FIFTY PONNDS.

Given at the Council Chamber in Dublin, the 23d Day of February, 1792.

Fitz-Gibbon, C. John Foſter. J. Parnell. Henry King. William Conyngham. James Cuff. J. Monck Maſon. R. Hobart. Arthur Wolfe. James Fitzgerald. Geo. Warde.

GOD Save the KING.

March 14, 1794.

THE SOCIETY OF UNITED IRISHMEN OF

DUBLIN,

TO THE PEOPLE OF IRELAND.

WE submitted to your consideration such a plan for your equal representation, as would, in our judgment, if carried into effect, give you your just and constitutional weight in the legislature. We exulted in the thought that our exertions had contributed to raise the public mind to that elevated point, from which it might view it's widely extended rights; from which it might discover the real insignificance of every proposal towards reform, that should not seek the full measure of justice; which should not give to all, who were in any degree bound by the law, the power of chusing those who made the law. We thought the simplicity of the Plan the best Test of it's honesty, and that it's appeal to the common sense of the nation rendered any explanation of it's principles unnecessary. We are, however, now called upon to justify it's primary principle by the objections, which have since been raised against it; and should we succeed, our triumph must be that of argument over invective, of reason over prejudice, and of justice over power.

It is an apprehension with some that should every man be allowed to vote for a representation in parliament, the monarchy and aristocracy of the Constitution would soon be overborne and destroyed by the exorbitant power and republican ſpirit of the democracy. Let it be remembered, that the Britiſh Conſtitution has amply provided againſt the probability of ſuch an event. It has appointed a ſole executive officer, inveſted with prerogatives to ſtrengthen the executive power, and with a certain portion of legiſlative authority to defend thoſe prerogatives. It has inſtituted a ſubſtantial ariſtocracy, not deriving all it's weight and authority merely from the king's patents, but hereditary, and poſſeſſing a maſs of property, by which, backed and ſupported, if neceſſary, by the executive prerogatives and legiſlative authority of the crown, it is enabled to withſtand the attacks of the democracy. Away then with this idle apprehenſion—Can any danger attach upon ſo much influence and ſo much power? On the contrary, can any thing ſhort of pure democracy maintain againſt them the integrity and independence of the Houſe of Commons?

But it is ſaid that the lower claſſes of the community, being without property, have no ſtake in the country, and therefore ought not to vote for any part of the legiſlature. In conſequence of the repreſentative ſyſtem every man is ſuppoſed to be either individually or by his delegate a party to making the laws, by which he is to be bound. * The elective right cannot therefore be denied

* Altho' this is at preſent only a *ſuppoſition*, yet there are ſtrong reaſons for believing that it was once a *fact*. Mr. Prynne, one of the moſt profound legal antiquarians, aſſerts, that before the 8th Hen. 6th ch. 7. every inhabitant and commoner in each County had a voice in the election of Knights, whether he were a freeholder or not." Brev. Parl. Red. p. 187. —Of the ſame opinion ſeems Whitelocke. 2d Whitel. p. 50.—It ſeems very conſiderably confirmed by the

on conſtitutional principle to any one; as they are bound by the laws as well as others. Laws operate on life, liberty, and property. Why is property repreſented? Becauſe it is valuable to the poſſeſſor, and may be affected by the law. Why ſhould liberty and life not be repreſented? Are they not more valuable to their poſſeſſor, and may they not alſo be affected by the law? Since liberty and Life are the moſt important objects of legiſlation, the poorer claſs have a right to ſome controul over the legiſlature, and it is juſt that they ſhould exerciſe it. The ſpirit of many of our laws is ariſtocratic, and by no means calculated for the protection of the poor. To paſs over the remarkable inſtances of the Game Laws and the Stamp Act, the latter of which, by operating on legal proceedings, ſhuts the door of juſtice againſt the poor, we ſhall refer to a much more important ſyſtem, our *criminal Code*. If the lower claſſes of the community had been repreſented in Parliament, when their neceſſities firſt urged them to inſurrection and outrage, under the denominations of White Boys and Defenders, Parliament would have enquired into and redreſſed their grievances, inſtead of making laws to puniſh them with death. The Acts, which are prohibited by many of our laws are crimes: but the puniſhments, inflicted by thoſe laws, are ſtill greater crimes. The reaſon of this diſproportion

word of the 7th Hen. 4. ch. 15.—And Sir Thomas Smyth in his commonwealth p. 37. has the following words "every Engliſhman is intended to be preſent in Parliament, either in perſon, or by procuration or attorney, of what pre-eminence, ſtate, dignity, or quality ſoever he be, from the prince to the LOWEST perſon in England, and the conſent of the Parliament is taken to be every man's conſent."

is, that the rich man is never guilty of sheep-stealing, and the poor man has no one to plead his cause in the senate.

If, however, it be a principle that no man, who does not contribute to the support of government, should be mediately or immediately concerned in legislation, such principle would be no exclusion of the poor, for they contribute in proportion to their means. The poorest man in the land pays taxes for his fire, his candle, for his potatoes, and his cloathing: and the poorer he is, the greater occasion he has for a vote to protect what little he has, which is necessary not to his qualification merely, but to his very existence. He has a property in his labour, and in the value it will bring in the market, the field, or the manufactory: a property, on account of it's smallness, of more real value to him than thousands of pounds to the rich and luxurious: a property, which must render him more interested in the honest disposal of the public money, since one additional tax may crush him, than those can be who receive that public money by virtue of places without employment and pensions without merit. Property is merely the collection of labour: it possesses the very same qualities before, as after, it is collected into a heap; and the scattered labour of the lowest ranks is as real, and ought to be as really represented as the most fixed and solid property. Reason, we think, says this; and sad experience has manifested, that giving political power exclusively to property collected, not to the mass of living labour, has been in all ages, and particularly in modern times, the true cause of feudality, of vassalage, and of aristocratic despotism.

It is also used as an argument, that altho' in theory every man has a right to vote, yet the exercise of that right among us would be impracticable or attended with outrage from the multitude of voters. To that we answer, that the practicability of the measure depends on a few regulations, which, we apprehend, could be easily contrived to render elections practicable and tranquil. Let there be a division of the kingdom into parts, sufficiently small, and, as nearly as possible, equal with respect to population, and let the several elections annually commence and conclude throughout the kingdom on one and the same day.

Some friends to universal suffrage in a new country urge a local objection to it's being applied to Ireland. They say that the lower classes of people in this country are peculiarly unfit for the exercise of suffrage on account of their extreme ignorance. We know of no description of people in this country are peculiarly unfit for the exercise of their rights: and if we did, we would fit them for it by giving it to them. What has made those classes so extremely ignorant? The privation of those rights, which, if enjoyed, would have procured them knowledge. Apply the reverse of that, which has debased, and it will exalt them. Give them the elective franchise, and let them exercise it directly. It is not just to judge of what the people would be, when embodied into the constitution of their country, from their present state of debasement, in which they feel themselves unconnected with it. We trust that our countrymen, even the poorest, who are now stigmatized with the appellations of Swine, Wretches, and Rabble, would, if restored to their rights, evince an elevation of sentiment, which, setting every species of corruption at defiance, must humble the pride of wealth by the superior lustre of virtuous poverty.

Indeed the local circumſtances ſeem to us rather in favour of introducing it into Ireland. We have lately had occaſion, in conſidering the Catholic claims. to examine into the foundations of government. The Catholic has taught all Ireland, that to be taxed or legiſlated for, without being repreſented, is an opppreſſion, which ſinks the ſufferer into a ſlave. He inſiſted on his right to the elective ſuffrage, becauſe he was bound by the laws, and contributed to the expences of the ſtate. The doctrine, once broached, can never be forgotten; and the remaining ſlave, whom reform ſhall not have raiſed to the rank of citizen, will remember the argument of the Catholic, and aſk himſelf "am I not bound by the laws; and "do I not, in my humble ſphere, contribute to "the expences of the ſtate? Why am I not re-"preſented? Is it not my right? and ſhall I not "inſiſt upon my right." Sooner or later the meaſure muſt come. The eternal principle of juſtice will be repeated in louder and louder tones, until at length it muſt be heard and obſerved. Why then not now? Why leave behind a ſource of new reforms, perhaps, of convulſions? If reform only communicate power to a greater number, and do not give liberty to all, it will only ſtrengthen the ruling, and weaken the oppreſſed body? ſo that when the ſlave ſhall have acquired ſufficient courage to ſpeak, the obſtinacy of the citizen will compel him to act. We cannot forget the language made uſe of to intimidate the Catholic from proſecuting his claims, and that thoſe very claims, ſhortly after having been rejected with ſcorn, was admitted with reſpect. The ſame line of prudence and wiſdom will, we are perſuaded, be purſued in the caſe of reform, whenever convincing proof of the public ſentiment ſhall be received on that ſubject, and the kingdom, by the reſtoration of universal suffrage, be delivered over to uninterrupted peace and happiness.

Contemplating this grateful prospect, we smile, with much internal satisfaction, on hearing those intemperate and abusive expressions, which the members of opposition make use of against this Society. We smile at their inability to conceal the vexation and disappointment they have felt on finding themselves forsaken by the People—(That people, whose majesty they insult, but whose forbearance they at the same time solicit,)—on finding themselves falling, like the ostentatious Balloon, from that height, to which they had risen by a sort of inflammable levity, and there sustained solely by the breath of popular favour. We smile at the curious coalition of political parties against our Society—to see them all club their wisdom and their wit, to manifest to the whole country that we are really formidable—but we are rather inclined to pity that forced fraternity, that monstrous conjunction which, in spite of the horror of instinct, and the antipathy of nature, can join in one common effort the highest Genius with the lowest Ribaldry—How great must be the panic that can unite such extremes! We can bear, as we have borne, the common place invective against this Society: but we feel some indignation, when they, who should look on themselves as the purchased property of the people; to whose fortune every man, even "*the Beggar on the Bridge,*" has contributed; whom the "*shouts of the Mob*" have raised to the height of their Fame—When such men inveigh against armed Beggary and Shabby Sedition, we cannot but remember a time, when the usual adjunct to their own names was "Shabby "and Seditious Incendiaries." It is not manly, it is not decorous to deal out this contumelious language againſt the great maſs of mankind. The uſe of contemptuous terms diſpoſes to contemptuous treatment, and thoſe, whom we vilify as Mob, we ſoon learn to ſlight as men. It is the unequal partition of rights, and what reſults from this, the arrogance of power, and the abaſement of poverty, which makes Mob, inſtigates to tumult, and goads to inſurrection. If the people were reſpected they would reverence the conſtituted authorities; but to gain this reſpect, they muſt poſſeſs thoſe rights, which are the prerogative of their nature, and the worth of manhood.

Oppoſition ſeem ſurpriſed that the people ſhould view their debates with indifference. We will tell them the reaſon. It is becauſe nothing paſſes of a nature to animate and intereſt that people—nothing, from which an individual can promiſe himſelf more happineſs, or the community more ſplendour—it is becauſe enthuſiaſm no longer lights up the countenance of Grattan, and ſwells every heart with ſomething great and good, and with a proſpect of ſomething greater and better—it is becauſe there appears no internal ſpring of action, no fixture of character; but good and bad qualities, as it were, *external*, and neither virtues nor vices their own. It is becauſe once in ſeven years the people are treated as Majeſty, and in the interval maltreated as Mob.

We have not in our Plan of Reform paled in little parks of ariſtocracy—Our Plan has not been deſcribed with a pair of compaſſes, nor have we defaced with childiſh circles the ſyſtem of nature, and the chart of the Conſtitution. There is no truth in any political ſyſtem, in which the Sun of Liberty is not placed in the centre, with knowledge to enlighten, and benevolence to warm and invigorate; with the ſame ray to gild the Palace and illuminate the Cottage. The

Earth moves ſaid Gallieo, and the Sun ſtands ſtill. He was impriſoned for the heretical aſſertion, for a libel againſt the laws of nature, and for exciting ſedition among the ſtars—But the Earth moves notwithſtanding; and in ſpite of fine, impriſonment, pillory and tranſportation, the Rights of Man are the immoveable centre of the Britiſh Conſtitution, that has hitherto regulated times and determined Revolutions.

CONSTITUTION

OF THE

SOCIETY OF UNITED IRISHMEN

OF THE CITY OF DUBLIN.

THE Society is conſtituted for the purpoſe of forwarding a brotherhood of affection, an identity of intereſts, a communion of rights, and an union of power, among Iriſhmen of all religious perſuaſions, and thereby obtaining an impartial and adequate repreſentation of the Nation in Parliament.

The members of this Society are either ordinary or honorary.

Such perſons only are eligible as honorary members, who have diſtinguiſhed themſelves by promoting the liberties of mankind, and are not inhabitants of Ireland.

Every candidate for admiſſion into the Society, whether as an ordinary or honorary member, ſhall be propoſed by two ordinary members, who ſhall ſign a certificate of his being, from their knowledge of him, a fit perſon to be admitted—that he has ſeen the teſt, and is willing to take it: This certificate, delivered to the Secretary, ſhall be read from the Chair at the enſuing meeting of the Society; and on the next ſubſequent night of meeting the Society ſhall proceed to the election.—The names and additions of the candidate, with the names of thoſe by whom he has been propoſed, ſhall be inſerted in the ſummons for the night of election.—The election, ſhall be conducted by ballot, and if one-fifth of the number of beans be black, the candidate ſtands rejected. The election, with reſpect to an ordinary member, ſhall be void, if he does not attend within four meetings afterwards, unleſs he can plead ſome reaſonable excuſe, for his abſence.

Every perſon elected a member of the Society, whether honorary or ordinary, ſhall previous to his admiſſion, take and ſubſcribe the following teſt:

"I *A. B.* in the preſence of God, do pledge "myſelf to my country, that I will uſe all my "abilities and influence in the attainment of "an impartial and adequate repreſentation of the "Iriſh nation in Parliament; and as a means "of abſolute and immediate neceſſity in the "eſtabliſhment of this chief good of Ireland, I "will endeavour, as much as lies in my ability, "to forward a brotherhood of affection, an iden-"tity of intereſts, a communion of rights, and "an union of power among Iriſhmen of all reli-"gious perſuaſions; without which every reform "in Parliament muſt be partial, not national, "inadequate to the wants, deluſive to the wiſhes, "and inſufficient for the freedom and happineſs "of this country.

A member of another Society of United Iriſhmen being introduced to the Preſident by a member of this Society, ſhall, upon producing a certificate ſigned by the Secretary, and ſealed with the Seal of the Society to which he belongs, and taking the before-mentioned teſt, be thereupon admitted to attend the ſittings of this Society.

The officers of the Society ſhall conſiſt of a Preſident, Treaſurer and Secretary, who ſhall be ſeverally elected every three months, viz. on every firſt night of meeting in the months of November, February, May and Auguſt; the election to be determined by each member preſent writing on a piece of paper the names of the object of his choice, and putting it into a box—The majority of votes shall decide—If the votes are equal, the President shall have a casting voice. No person shall be capable of being re-elected to any office for the quarter next succeeding the determination of his office. In case of an occasional vacancy in any office by death or otherwise, the Society shall on the next night of meeting, elect a person to the same for the remainder of the quarter.

The Society shall meet on every second Friday night—oftener if necessary.—The Chair shall be taken at eight o'Clock from 29th September to 25th March, and at nine o'Clock from 25th March to 29th September. Fifteen members shall form a quorum. No new business shall be introduced after ten o'Clock.

Every respect and deference shall be paid to the President—his chair shall be raised three steps above the seats of the members—the Treasurer and Secretary shall have seats under him, two steps above the seats of the members.—On his rising from his Chair and taking off his hat, there must be silence, and the members be seated. —He shall be judge of order and propriety, be impowered to direct an apology, and to fine refractory members in any sum not above one Crown.—If the member refuse to pay the fine, or make the apology, he is thereupon expelled from the Society.

There shall be a Committee of Constitution, of Finance, of Correspondence, and of Accommodation.—The Committee of Constitution shall consist of nine members, that of Finance of seven members, that of Correspondence of five members.—Each Committee shall, independent of occasional reports, make general reports on every quarterly meeting. The Treasurer shall be under the direction of the Committee of Finance, and the Secretary under the direction of the Committee of correſpondence. The election for Committees ſhall be on every quarterly meeting, and decided by the majority of votes.

In order to defray the neceſſary expences, and eſtabliſh a fund for the uſe of the Society, each ordinary member ſhall on his election pay to the Treaſurer, by thoſe who propoſed him, one Guinea admiſſion fee, and alſo one Guinea annually, by half yearly payments, on every firſt night of meeting in November and May; the firſt payment thereof to be on the firſt night of meeting in November 1792. On every quarterly meeting following, the names of the defaulters, as they appear in the Treaſury-book, ſhall be read from the chair—If any member after the ſecond reading neglect to pay his ſubſcription, he ſhall be excluded the Society, unleſs he can ſhew ſome reaſonable excuſe for his default.

The Secretary ſhall be furniſhed with the following ſeal, viz. a Harp—at the top "*I am* "*new ſtrung*;" at the bottom "*I will be heard*;" and on the exergue "*Society of United Iriſhmen* "*of Dublin*."

No motion for an alteration of, or addition to the conſtitution ſhall be made but at the quarterly meetings, and notice of ſuch motion ſhall be given fourteen days previous to thoſe meetings—If upon ſuch motion the Society ſhall ſee ground for the propoſed alteration or addition, the ſame ſhall be referred to the proper committee, with inſtructions to report on the next night of meeting their opinion thereon; and upon ſuch report the queſtion ſhall be decided by the Society.

THOMAS MUIR.

TO THE SOCIETY OF UNITED IRISHMEN OF DUBLIN.

AT this period, to expreſs to you my zeal in your cauſe, and my attachment to your Society would be ſuperfluous and unbecoming. Upon the eve, of being, perhaps for ever, ſeparated from this country and from civilized life, I depart in the firm conviction, that your future proceedings, will be correſponding to the preceding, that your conduct will be marked by that calm but dignified fortitude, which becomes the adherents of freedom, that, trampling upon intrigue, and triumphing over deſpotiſm you muſt finally accompliſh the emancipation of Ireland.

In your immortal addreſs, which I had the honour of preſenting to the firſt Convention in Scotland, you have ſaid " away from us and " from our children, thoſe puerile antipathies, " ſo unworthy of the manhood of nations, which " inſulate individuals as well as countries, and " drive the citizen back to the ſavage. We " eſteem and we reſpect you." Let me in the name of my country preſume to entreat the continuance of your eſteem, for the great maſs of the people in Scotland. They deſerve your eſteem. In the holy cauſe of national freedom, they are actuated by the ſame ſpirit which animates you. Towards you their hearts burn with affection. Thoſe barriers which a cruel policy had ſet up, to ſeparate nation from nation, are now broken down. Of titled diſtinction and of haughty opulence, they cannot boaſt, but they poſſeſs a better treaſure—VIRTUE—VIRTUE the only ſure pledge of the exiſtence and of the continuation of patriotifm. With clean hands, and with pure hearts, they are worfhippers along with you in that temple which is truly Catholic.—The ample earth its area, and the arch of Heaven its dome.

Permit me to congratulate your Society, upon the incorruptible integrity of its members, who have ftood the teft of perfecution. Thefe individuals are both a pledge for, and a fpecimen of the general body. Their fufferings impofe a folemn obligation upon you, to adhere to that caufe, of which they have been the firft martyrs. Not difcouraged, by what they at prefent endure, you will perfevere and imitate their example, and in exile, in the receffes of a dungeon, if need be, you will exhibit yourfelves worthy of the honour of having been the affociates of James Napper Tandy, of Simon Butler of Oliver Bond, and of James Reynolds.

To have been introduced to you by Archibald Hamilton Rowan, conftitutes my higheft pride. To participate with him in common fuffering conftitutes my beft diftinction.

THOMAS MUIR.

Portfmouth, 10*th March,* 1794.

Surprize Tranfport, for Botany Bay.

The following papers were accidently omitted in their proper places.

June 22, 1792.

ARCHIBALD HAMILTON ROWAN, in the Chair.

JOHN BOURKE, Secretary.

A COMMITTEE appointed by this Society to take into confideration the profecution of James Napper Tandy, purfuant to an order of the Houfe of Commons, for an alledged breach of privilege, and his acquittal thereof by his country, having prefented their report, it was thereupon.

RESOLVED UNANIMOUSLY, That the Houfe of Commons having in the firft inftance inflicted punifhment without proof of guilt, and in the fecond, profecuted for imputed offence, when twelve refpectable citizens on oath have not been able to find proof fufficient to convict; and having thus attempted to add the penalties of the law to the exercife of an arbitrary power; this Society do congratulate the people of Ireland, that the integrity and difcernment of a Dublin Jury, have interfered to protect the caufe of juftice and the Conftitution in the perfon of a fellow citizen.

November, 16*th*, 1792.

To THOMAS BRAUGHAL, Esq. Chairman of the MEETING of CATHOLICS of DUBLIN.

SIR,

THE Society of United Irishmen of Dublin, have received your communication of the proceedings of the Catholics of this City, with great satisfaction.

From our zeal to promote the restoration of Catholic Rights, we can derive no merit as we are actuated no less by considerations of interest, than those of duty.

In sound policy, Catholic and Protestant Rights are the same. It was by weak and wicked policy that they were disunited, however, our cases are not so very different, for they exhibit little more than an equal distribution of wrongs.

You certainly reflect our sentiments while you reclaim the radical principle of political association, that a delegated body can not, without usurpation, exercise the power of annihilating their creators, and we lament that it is not possible instantly to extirpate, along with the precedent, the very memory of the act which disfranchises the mass of the people.

We are with all due respect,

your most obedient humble servants,

WILLIAM DRENNAN, *Chairman*

December 20th, 1793.

THE SOCIETY OF UNITED IRISHMEN OF DUBLIN.

THE Society taking into consideration the oppressive attempt in Edinburgh to stifle the voice of the people, through the British Convention, and the spirited and truly patriotic resistance to that attempt.

RESOLVED, that all or any of the members of the British Convention, and of the patriotic Societies, which delegated members to that Convention, shall be received as brothers and members of this Society.

MAGNA EST VERITAS

ET

PRÆVALEBIT.

www.ingramcontent.com/pod-product-compliance
Lightning Source LLC
Chambersburg PA
CBHW030821270326
41928CB00007B/843
9783337126247